The Great Awakening

THE REVELATIONS OF CONNIE ANN VALENTI

DONALD MARINELLI

Fulton Books
Meadville, PA

Published by Fulton Books 2022

ISBN 979-8-88505-013-5 (paperback)
ISBN 979-8-88505-014-2 (digital)

Printed in the United States of America

Prologue

There is no timetable when it comes to the process of revelation. Revelation occurs when it occurs. Revelations are seldomly effortlessly discernible, perfectly syntactic, easily defensible, or corroborated by prior history, explanation, or dogma. Stated succinctly: revelation is seldom pretty but always challenging, stimulating, and, more often than not, enlightening.

The question existing among many regarding Connie Ann Valenti is rather straightforward: who is she and what is she? We know who she is as a human being: a God-fearing, loving wife, mother, and grandmother who is endowed with great spiritual blessings. That leads us to ask a rather simple and direct question: Is she a prophetess, a mystic, a medium, a seer? What exactly?

We can discount thinking of her solely as a medium. Mediums serve as intermediaries between spirits of the deceased and living human beings. Mediums often proffer communication through the act of channeling. Connie Ann Valenti's gifts, however, are not dependent upon external triggers, such as questions from the living to those who have transitioned to the spiritual realm.

A prophet is one who delivers the Word of God by means of direct revelation. Prophetic utterances can deal with spiritual entities, incarnated beings, the church or churches, society, the planet, heaven, the universe—anything within and without it. Prophecy does not always refer to the future.

A mystic is a person who, by contemplation and self-surrender, obtains unity with, or absorption, into higher consciousness: the spiritual apprehension of truths beyond the intellect. In that regard, we can say Connie Ann Valenti possesses mystical capabilities. The difference is that this is seldom—if ever—entirely volitional on her part. This "spiritual apprehension of truths" comes over her without forethought or planning. It just happens. The message (and messengers) decide when and where to make themselves manifest through Mrs. Valenti.

A seer is one who sees with spiritual eyes, serving as a perceiver of hidden truths, which are oftentimes obscure to others. In that regard, a seer serves as an interpreter and clarifier of eternal truths. A seer is able to foresee the future from the vantage point of both the past and the present. This can occur via channeling—the act whereby a mental/spiritual bridge connects the temporal physical world to higher or parallel dimensional consciousness.

In light of the definitions above, we can and should look upon Connie Ann Valenti as part prophetess/part seer/part mystic. This is because her revelations encompass the very detailed origins of all that exists spiritually and physically, clarification of the celestial hierarchy, history of humankind, the purpose of life and reincarnation, the roles and responsibilities of the protagonists and antagonists of the Old and New Testaments, the power of prayer, and the foretelling of Earth's end-times.

What we do know about revelation in general is that the term is used to refer to the process by which God, or higher consciousness, reveals knowledge of Him/Itself, His/its will, and His/its divine providence to human beings. The revelations of Connie Ann Valenti definitely qualify as such.

The revelations contained in this volume provide reconfirmation of much revealed in *The Story of Creation*, but also many new startling, powerful, and mystifying revelations. These new revelations further explain and clarify the host of celestial entities introduced and revealed in the first book—further clarifying origins, purposes, interactions, and interventions with humanity (good and bad) as well as exposing truths behind alien abduction, alien-human experimentation, and the panoply of creatures inherent in human mythology, folklore, and legend.

Our challenge as readers of these revelations is contained within St. Paul's guidance in Thessalonians 5:19–21, "Despise not prophecies, but prove all things. Hold fast that which is good." This is clearly easier said than done because exactly how does one "prove" revelations?

There are no promised revelations that will neatly explain, clarify, correct, or tie together mysteries that have beset humankind for millennia. Many of Connie Ann Valenti's revelations in fact raise as many questions as they potentially explain. The epilogue to this book that I have written strives to identify how Connie Ann Valenti's revelations reflect, address, and support much of humankind's spiritual, social, philosophical, and psychological ontology. It also spotlights many of the new mysteries and challenges these revelations have brought forth.

Many of these new revelations illuminate brilliantly and succinctly things never before considered or understood. Readers of *The Story of Creation*—and this follow-up work—will note and identify much existing in the Old and New Testaments. Many things will become clearer as a result while many new perplexing mysteries have been presented.

Perhaps the true power of these revelations is the degree to which they spur each individual's quest to understand who we are, what we are, and the meaning of our existence.

The Progression of Creation from The One to the Heavenly Father

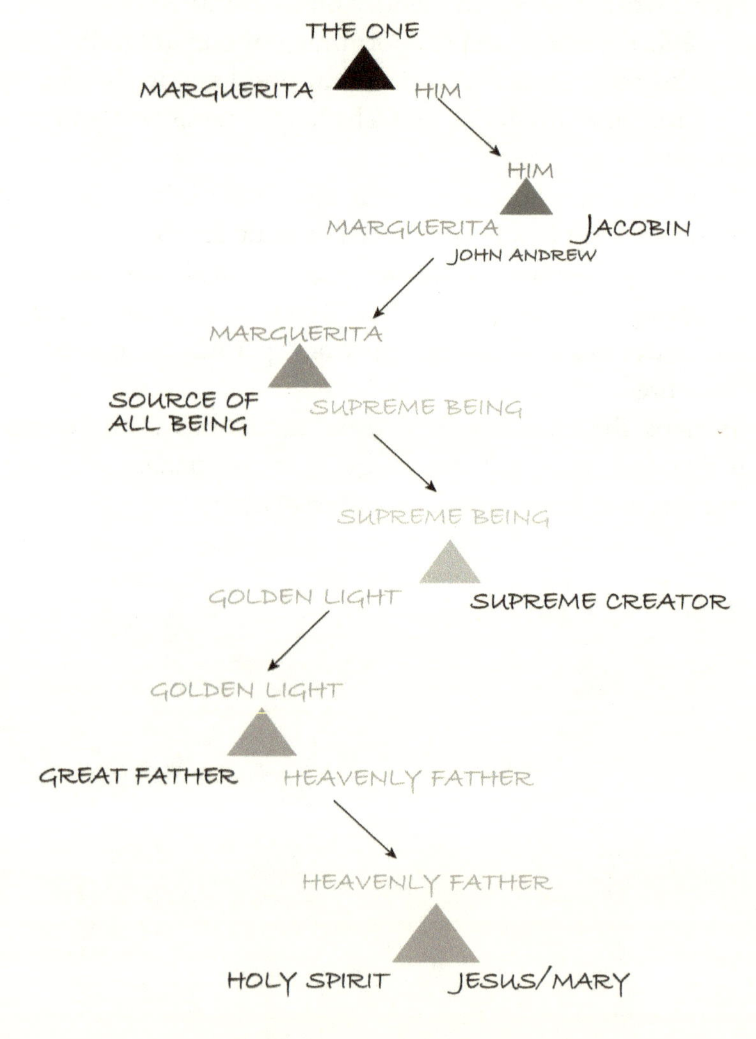

Introduction

Where the book *The Story of Creation* ended, we begin with new revelation and, therefore, greater understanding about Lucifer, enlightenment regarding other life in the universe, the eternal struggle between good and evil, and the final stage of life on the Earth before the final judgment.

An entity named "The One" brings forth and encompasses the ultimate source of life. The One is an entity made up of powerful eternal energies. Before the creation of our universe, one of those energies appeared unexpectedly in his own unique form. As described in the prior Connie Ann Valenti text, *The Story of Creation*, this entity (who we have named Marguerita because of her pearl-like origins) is the spiritual being who emerged from within The One.

The One had to release her, knowing full well she would need to exist until the end of what would come to be known to humankind as "time." Once that culmination occurs, Marguerita will return to The One because her energy will once again be needed to fill the void her origination created within The One.

Marguerita can be considered the mother of all creation, the spiritual progenitor who gave life to five higher spiritual beings. She closely monitored the whole creative process, providing additional energy when needed. Her support and guidance sustained her, kept her attuned and wholly attentive to the unfolding cosmos. While overseeing this creation, gestating within her was a being we will refer to by the name of Jacobin.

Marguerita did not want to leave The One, knowing her appearance meant she would become part of end-times and final judgment. She cried out to no one—and yet to everyone—that the truths she had come to reveal would not be believed. When Marguerita first came forth from the light of The One coursing through the darkness, it was into what would become a spiritual universe.

Together with one of the five higher spiritual beings, appropriately named the Great Father, he and Marguerita completed the second phase of creation by giving life to another four spiritual beings. These spiritual beings are the Brothers. Together with the five higher spiritual entities, the four Brothers were expected to live in peace forever. Unfortunately, that did not happen.

Each of these celestial beings was endowed with an important responsibility to accomplish within a divine plan established for the universe. Unfortunately, when time came for creation of the four Brothers, the energy of the Great Father was nearly spent. Consequently, the Brothers did not receive the proper amount of energy that should have been given to them. This absence would have a direct impact on their yet undetected fifth brother—the entity that would become our Heavenly Father.

Each of the Heavenly Father's four brothers was given a planetary system. They reside in another part of our universe together with their subjects. It is important to understand they do not rule as gods.

The four Brothers inhabit similar energy orbits circling their designated planets; planets that did not move at first. The Brothers believed they were each solitary inhabitants of the universe, much like humans perceived themselves to be solitary intelligent life in the universe—at least until recently.

Let us then review the various phases of creation. The One, spawning of Marguerita, and creation of the initial cadre of five celestial beings constitutes the first phase. Creation of the Brothers, an act initiated by Marguerita and the Great Father, constitute the second phase. The creation of the Heavenly Father and his various progeny, of which humanity is a key component, mark the third phase of creation.

The Heavenly Father is the most mysterious and perhaps misunderstood person in this entire story, created after the life forces of the Brothers and their subjects were activated. Together with the entity called "Him"—a name derived from the vibrational sound of his being—our Heavenly Father accompanied Marguerita like a shadow from The One.

Our Heavenly Father—the fifth of five offspring from The One, the Great Father, and Marguerita—is very distinct from his brethren. Unlike his four brothers, our Heavenly Father is a God and is to be worshipped as God. There was no god before Him for humankind, nor will there be a god for us after him. He is the only one in our universe to be given that title. He should be obeyed and revered as a deity.

The planet Earth was given to the Heavenly Father as his kingdom, albeit designated eventually for Lucifer. As it turns out, Earth was not created in a perfect state. It was and remains "imperfect." To understand this imperfection, we need to focus upon an archangel by the original name of Lucifer.

PART 1

Lucifer

Lucifer's Beginnings

The energy from supernatural beings to create Earth existed before Lucifer arrived. This same energy circling Earth keeps Lucifer bound to it. This energy came from the Golden Light through the Great Father. Both have had a very active role in the creation of this new universe.

Lucifer's development, described in detail in *The Story of Creation*, remains immensely complicated. Lucifer does not have many memories, but there is a significant one with ramifications for all humanity.

Lucifer was an archangel created to supplement the energy of the Heavenly Father, a divine entity who had not developed fully, a spiritual being that needed additional energy to sustain Him. Because of the Heavenly Father's curiosity, the growth of both Lucifer and Mother Nature (an essential part of Lucifer's being) was also stunted. Lucifer had not been given enough time to develop into the pure spirit he was created to be. It was one of many missteps in the process of creation.

When Lucifer emerged from the "womb" of Marguerita, she appeared sad and distressed. In her core being, she knew her maternal labors were not yet complete. "No, there is another one," she announced, calling forth from within her an additional son, a fraternal twin to be named Jacobin, but he refused to come. Lucifer, on the other hand, had been most willing and came forth freely.

When his birth was complete, Lucifer swore to Marguerita he would always stay with her. He said, "You conceived me. I shall fill the world with fire." Marguerita began to weep. She called out to Jacobin yet again, but he still would not come forth. He explained, "It would be wrong for me to leave now. I should not be born at the same time as Lucifer." Consequently, he remained with Marguerita—for the time being.

While there is much about the divine plan we do not know or understand, we do know that even before the commencement of time, a battle between good and evil had been taking place. Motivated by jealousy and undertaken with trickery, Lucifer was able to pilfer most of the Heavenly Father's energy. This was the very energy needed to sustain the Heavenly Father and which was Lucifer's primary responsibility.

While Lucifer was resting, some of the archangels around the Heavenly Father pilfered energy from him and channeled it to Lucifer. This allowed Lucifer to become ever stronger, increasing his daring and fueling his arrogance. Because the Heavenly Father lost so much energy, it became difficult for him to create Earth as Lucifer's future dominion. This was an act he should have been able to accomplish by simply cupping his hands together; but owing to this weakness, he needed to rest often.

A glutton for energy, Lucifer experienced great frustration because of his inability to siphon energy from the Heavenly Father's Brothers because they were created differently than the Heavenly Father. If Lucifer had been able to do that, humanity would have been in even worse trouble. That this did not occur is confirmation divine providence always works on our behalf, albeit oftentimes contrary to our human wisdom.

The Golden Light, one of the original progenies from The One and Marguerita, knew something had to be done to stop Lucifer. Otherwise, the Heavenly Father could be harmed in some unknown way. As a result, the Golden Light emitted a terrible piercing sound throughout the entire universe. This same terrible piercing sound would occur later in time when Jesus was crucified. It will be heard one final time during the world's end—a siren call immediately preceding the last judgment.

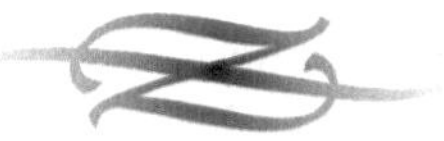

Rejection of Mother Nature

Lucifer heard this terrifying sound and became concerned it might have meant the Heavenly Father had become aware of his thievery. Although Lucifer did not realize it immediately, there were two distinct sides to his ontology, i.e., fundamental elements to his being. Lucifer's other side goes by the classic name and descriptor of Mother Nature. Lucifer and Mother Nature were both archangelic entities brought together into a single supernatural entity.

Upon hearing the cry from the Golden Light, Lucifer blamed it on Mother Nature. The Heavenly Father believed him. The Golden Light then injected specific energy into the Heavenly Father to usher him into another hibernating deep sleep. This was done to make sure Lucifer would be unable to take any more energy from him for a long time.

When Mother Nature was created, she was given knowledge to assist in the development of Earth, although she did not know the origins of this gift. She generously gave her design to the Heavenly Father hoping to convince him that Lucifer was capable of changing. Unfortunately, that will never happen.

The Source of All Being tried to comfort Mother Nature by giving her the ability to create, but she was never again to come near Lucifer. At that moment, the Golden Light inspired the Heavenly Father to create Earth, a world where Lucifer could be sent. Mother Nature also wanted to help in the creation of the Earth, but Lucifer paid no attention when Mother Nature asked to help design Earth.

Earth was very beautiful. That was until Lucifer covered it with evil. It was the origin of hate, an expression and attitude that did not exist previously. There is a love-hate relationship between Lucifer and Mother Nature: three-fourths hate, one fourth love. If the fallen angels in service to Lucifer had not been reined in by the Source of All Being, evil would have spread much more rapidly over all the Earth. Because of free will, the Source of All Being could not stop this attitudinal pandemic, though he did succeed in slowing it down. If this had not occurred, life on Earth would have essentially ended.

Despite their problems, Mother Nature loved Lucifer. She wanted him to have the beautiful planet she believed he desired and deserved. She hoped it might change his feelings about her, that they would come together, but the "bad blood" between them remained. His words had stung to her very core and made her feel unwanted. It hurt deeply every time Lucifer taunted her. Whenever she tried to reach out to him, he would repeat the same spiteful mantra: "Be gone. I do not want you or need you. I am my Father's son."

Her ready retort was always, "You will be sorry until the day you are destroyed." To this prophetic warning, he would just laugh and fall into deep slumber. Lucifer and Mother Nature were intrinsically attached. They possessed a modicum of respect for one another, but love was never seen nor heard between them.

Despite their sibling sustenance, the Heavenly Father decided it was time for them to be separated. Mother Nature disagreed vehemently. She cried out, "I must be with him." To which the Heavenly Father replied, "No, he shall be like a son to me." In that sense, Lucifer can rightly be considered the eldest son of the Heavenly Father.

Mother Nature wept and cried out, "But I am alone." The Heavenly Father did not hear her. Lucifer did. He mocked her, "Be gone. I do not need you, nor want you, nor desire you to be a part of me." They were bound to one another by a cord of life, but Lucifer managed to push her away. The Heavenly Father realized later this decision may not have been the best.

Mother Nature loved Lucifer, but she was always rejected by him. She noticed when Lucifer was taking life-sustaining energy from the Heavenly Father. The other angels of the Heavenly Host recognized this as well, but they had no reason to think it was wrong because Lucifer took it without the Heavenly Father objecting or complaining. They all believed and accepted there was a symbiotic relationship between them.

Lucifer Cut from Heavens

In a pitiful scene, Mother Nature cried out to the Heavenly Father on behalf of Lucifer. "He cannot be by himself!" The Heavenly Father still loved Lucifer, such that He was only half-listening to Mother Nature. She was receiving additional information from the higher, more ancient spiritual entities on how Earth should be created. She did not realize they were inspiring her.

The Heavenly Father was concerned not only about creating a kingdom that would please Lucifer, but also how to quickly create both it and the human souls he would endow as his subjects. It had to be a good match. An important question was whether these newly corporeal souls would be able to adjust to Earth's material atmosphere and coexist with Lucifer.

And so, after millions—or maybe even billions—of years together, Lucifer had to be cut from the heavens by the Heavenly Father. He was given Earth on which to reign as spiritual sovereign. When Earth was finished, the Heavenly Father covered Lucifer almost completely with a shell of protective energy. He said, "Lucifer, I give this kingdom to you with many angels and great beauty."

When Lucifer was cut from the heavens, the Heavenly Father gave him these and other energies. It was to prevent other angels from overtaking him, while enabling him to communicate with human beings, and to ultimately rule the Earth.

In many respects, he became more powerful than the Heavenly Father. He could have become ruler of the universe. In hindsight and perspective, the Heavenly Father should not have given humanity to Lucifer. There could very well be other reasons. Fortunately, Lucifer did not realize what power had been given to him.

There is a second memory Lucifer will never forget. While he was descending to Earth, he heard the Heavenly Father say, "I am giving you free will. This will be your kingdom. I will prepare souls to send to you. Teach them about my love for them. I will give them free will and provide a guardian angel to each of them. This is where and how you must prove your love for me."

Lucifer did not pay much attention to what the Heavenly Father said because he had taken so much energy from the Heavenly Father that he had become very much his equal. From the beginning, Lucifer had called out to the universe to make himself known. He wondered if there were other lives out there. He was not aware of how far his "voice" would travel. Neither he, nor the Heavenly Father, realized other lives did exist in the form of the Brothers' individual realms.

The truth is, the Heavenly Father did not see what was happening. The Heavenly Father wanted to believe his son, Lucifer, would return to him, seeking forgiveness for his arrogance, pride, and thievery. If this had occurred, all-encompassing peace and perfection would have been restored to the Earth. The Heavenly Father's love for Lucifer had blinded Him. He could no longer do anything to rein in his wayward destructive elder son. The energy Lucifer stole from the Heavenly Father, he used to control Earth, even aspiring to influence life on other planets.

Even though Lucifer was created out of love, a major part of him was filled with anger and a desire for absolute power. If he had done what was right, the Heavenly Father would have continued to create Lucifer's universe in accord with his original vision. Lucifer was given that ability, but it did not happen because of the anger, hatred, and mistrust that generated. If Lucifer had used his gifts for the purposes for which they were given, our planet would now be much different. It would more closely resemble heaven, rather than hell. The milk of kindness does not cover the wrath of fire.

Much troubles Lucifer since he screamed wildly as he fell to Earth after being cut from heaven. His evil energy was the source of his scream. It polluted the entire universe and remained there. Even though Lucifer must depend on the fallen angels, especially three or four powerful archangels who followed him to Earth, he did not trust them. He feared they might try to overthrow him, even though he knew they could never prevail.

Lucifer's newly-found anger brought him comfort. It spread over a universe where anger had never existed. He was the first being to experience anger and express it. It exists throughout the universe and will never be extinguished until the final judgment. Anger is the source of so much evil. The higher spiritual beings would like to dilute it, but they are not allowed to interfere in the Heavenly Father's realm.

Lucifer's primary motivation is that he wants to be—and sometimes does believe—he is our God. To try to prove it, he places his mark on us when we are first sent to Earth. His greatest fear is truth, especially the truth about him. There is a reason why he is referred to as the God of Darkness, both in heaven and on Earth.

In his rage, Lucifer releases anger to devastate Earth. Fortunately, a newly created band of angels prevents it. He is very angry at the Heavenly Father when he should be concerned at what he, himself, had done. He is furious more human beings have not followed him. He is angry at everything. Supernatural restraint will stop him from destroying the world, but when he is finally able to break away, Earth will be divided into good and bad. No one will listen to him.

Evil is like a virus. The angrier Lucifer gets, the more negative energy he expels and, ironically, the weaker he becomes. It has reached a point where even fallen angels are angry at Lucifer. They do not trust him anymore. Akin to how the sight of blood can confuse the mind of man, so it is that fallen angels are unable to understand these revelations of truth.

The scream of Lucifer contributed to the corruption of the universe and has caused him to rest more, thereby restraining some of the evil emanating from his existence. As a result of his scream, the planets of our solar system are moving out of line, thus starting the countdown to end-times.

The Heavenly Father installed a barrier so Lucifer could not hear his own scream as he fell to Earth. The Heavenly Father should not have created this barrier. It has protected Lucifer in ways not intended. Regardless, Lucifer will soon hear his own scream for the first time. It would have been even stronger if Marguerita had given him all the energy she could have. She decided to save some for what she knew Jacobin had to do.

Creation of Human Beings for Lucifer

With unseen assistance from higher celestial beings possessing the distinct energy needed to create a life-form distinct from the sentient spiritual entities already created, the Heavenly Father established a methodology and process for just such development on Earth. He had already determined he would give them a gift, a capability no other created entity had yet received. It would be called "free will."

This can be discerned from the fact that human souls were not given to Lucifer immediately. The Great Father, a behind-the-scenes celestial influencer, believed he needed more time to reconcile what Lucifer had done and how he might change his ways. Yet it was up to the Heavenly Father to initiate the creation and granting of human souls on Earth to Lucifer.

The creation of human life by the Heavenly Father can be described as an experiment entwined within a mystery far beyond human comprehension. Consigning his very own human creations to the care and oversight of Lucifer begs the question: Why would there be any reason for divinity to experiment? We might accurately posit this in the form of a thesis: If given free will by God, would humanity remain one with God, or would humanity want to live like God?

But first, we need to understand the temporal dynamic of creation. For instance, it needs to be appreciated that animals were created before humans, also as spiritual beings. They were all connected to the Heavenly Father via a beautiful golden light, a radiant source of comfort and peace. At first, there were only animals on this beautiful planet called Earth. They were spiritual beings similar to those created and existing throughout the universe among the Brothers' various realms.

When humans were subsequently created, they existed as unique but undeveloped spiritual beings. An energy of love existed between human souls, though they did not communicate directly with one another. Instead, communication between them existed as a state of perpetual accord and ecstasy.

We human beings, the Heavenly Father's followers, are distinctly different from the subjects of the other four Brothers. Unlike their followers, human beings residing on the surface of Earth became both spiritual and physical beings.

Animals and human beings recognized each other's uniqueness and enjoyed each other's spiritual beauty. The animals and human beings loved and cared for one another. They shared common love for the Heavenly Father.

During the very long stage of development, from spiritual to corporeal existence, man was ultimately endowed with a brain. It was provided as a gift, the aim being for humans to think and decide for themselves. The Great Father was the instigator of this evolution. Spiritual man had the potential for a brain, but physical man received it because we had to have a brain to make good decisions. Because of this change, Lucifer cannot force us to follow him. He lost what he thought he had won because we remain free to follow the laws, guidance, and mercy of the Heavenly Father.

Human beings were created with both male and female characteristics. The male part gives us strength; the female part gives us intelligence and care. In the beginning, the Heavenly Father determined the kind of mixture we would be given. Endowed with free will, however, and with previous lifetimes of experience in our spiritual DNA when we return to Earth to begin another life, we choose the proportions we want our body to be. Animals do not have that choice because their souls are different.

Human Development

We know the internal structure of Earth is layered in spherical shells: an outer silicate solid crust, a highly viscous asthenosphere and mantle, a liquid outer core that is much less viscous than the mantle, and a solid inner core. What we have yet to realize, however, is that the Earth is also comprised of various spiritual spheres. In the same way that humanity began as purely spiritual beings who then morphed into a combination of physicality and spirituality, so it was with our planet.

There are seven spherical levels encompassing the Earth. These spherical levels begin at the Earth's core. Each level possesses its own beauty, designed by Mother Nature, and is best understood as a consciousness-raising ladder. The knowledge of each participant increased with each level achieved. All souls originated from the twelve groups the Heavenly Father intended to give to Lucifer.

On level one, the soul learns basic lessons of existence. A special great angel was created to watch over the process on the first level. This is the level where one learns the basics of existence. This angel's divine responsibility was to learn to love fully the spiritual inhabitants of this domain. Although souls do not realize it, it is there that the gift of free will begins to be instilled in them. Existence alone suffices; there is no need for food.

When each soul manifested what was expected of it on the first level, the second level of this progressive transformation was initiated. The great angel guiding the soul's development accompanied it, uniting with another great angel on this second level. First though, this great angel shed a portion of its energy so that a measure of it remained behind to watch over the first level. This amalgamation of angelic energy continued with angels on each level until ultimately only one great angel was there to oversee the seventh level. Lesser angels remained on the prior six levels to protect them from Lucifer's desire to collect energy left behind.

The six angels, one from each level, grew as they ascended to the seventh level. They learned much about humanity. This cumulative knowledge will play an important role at the end of time. It is a responsibility we do not fully understand. These angels do not communicate with one another, but they serve an integral role in the development of human souls. In that process, they have been very loyal. They have done what was required of them by protecting souls.

On the second level, the soul is bathed in a golden light to prevent evil from influencing it during its spiritual evolution. On this level, the soul's awareness of its surroundings and its ongoing journey become manifest.

On the third level, souls began to understand the mind given to them. On the fourth level, they learned how to use it. On the fifth level, it all came together. Souls understood what it meant to be spiritual beings and how to live life as intended.

On the sixth level, beneath the surface of Earth, there exists underground cities designed by the Brothers—thought to be gods by early human beings. Much is stored on that level. Until now, these inhabitants have been unaware of the other five levels.

There is no natural light on the sixth level, even though some people are already living there. The person who discovered it, perhaps from Atlantis, constructed it as a place of freedom and safety for a select group of people. The occupants of this level possess great intelligence, wealth, and positions of power. Some of their children have been born through experiments performed on Earth.

They do not always want to live with those children. Some have been placed in a different part of the sixth level. These children look different because of the atmosphere in which they live. Their minds will devolve over a long period of time. Some children who are born naturally will grow smaller and smaller. Their intelligence will decrease. For those who are created artificially, however, the plan is to instill in them the ever-greater strength desired and needed by firm rulers.

The combined energy of the six levels is so strong it must ultimately be destroyed. Angels have been preselected to destroy the inside of Earth while the sun destroys the outside. That amount of energy must never be seen again. At the same time, Lucifer is angry from losing so much of his energy through his hatred and acts of destruction. He does not realize what he is doing to himself.

In time, man will discover the fifth and sixth levels of Earth. Many of their natural elements still exist. With the development of amazing new technologies, humanity will learn how these spirits evolved and lived. They will go back in time to capture every spoken word and thought in the universe. There are two hidden ways to gain access to this subterranean level. One is through a high mountain; the other is underneath an ocean. These access points will be discovered when the Earth's axis changes.

The angels from those levels of Earth are all connected to one another now. At the end of time, they will leave those levels and become a strong life force and ball of fire. They will cleanse each level where energies are left over from different souls passing through them. In the beginning, man was nurtured by the angels created for our benefit, but we have not yet learned how to fully utilize them.

For the rulers of the sixth domain, concern is centered on the seventh level of the planet, i.e., the planetary surface where we reside. It is the place where humans learn all they need to know.

The Book of Revelation tells us two will come to save all that was placed in the world by the heavens, not realizing how important it is. When the time comes to reveal the truth, they will do what is necessary with this energy. If evil continues to exist, they will institute goodness throughout the entire universe. Marguerita and Jacobin are "the two who will come."

Human spirits were scattered in different parts of the world. Some lived in warm climates, and others where it was cold. Various circumstances caused them to start using their minds more. They ate raw flesh at first because they liked the taste of blood. But when they experienced fire and the warmth it gave, they discovered they could burn flesh to give it a different taste, finding that preferable.

Final Step of Preparation

The seventh level is where the final battles will be fought and where all truths will be revealed. It is where life has evolved from an entirely spiritual existence to a combined spiritual/physical existence. It is also where Earth (as we know it) will be destroyed in the future. Fortunately, for all humanity, it is also where Jesus marked Earth with his blood.

The chosen and privileged people of this seventh level, those who are part of this great secret society, will be told when to retreat into the vast fortress hidden from sight on the Earth's sixth level. This elect group is comprised primarily of third-generation scientists and biologists who want to reduce the population of the planet. Lucifer is their leader and inspiration. They have started many wars and are now turning to biological warfare. They have chosen to use a plague. It will be a catastrophe affecting the entire world. A terrible plague will change the structure of Earth. Bodies will lay in the streets. Blood will run in the gutters. The stench will be horrible. This last cycle of life has just begun. We do not know how long it will last.

In the spiritual evolution of humanity, certain souls did not want to take life from others. In fact, in the beginning, humans did not eat or drink. They were sustained by returning to the Heavenly Father for renewal. They could sustain themselves in that way alone: not needing any other form of renewal. They felt this way because they had coexisted in heaven with the Heavenly Father far longer than they had coexisted with Lucifer on Earth. They were able to think and reason more clearly. They knew they had free will and did not have to stay with Lucifer. They also knew free will had been given to them so they could praise and love the Heavenly Father. They did not believe they had to follow Lucifer's plan or direction for them. Many fled into the depths of the Earth.

The seventh level is where Jesus marked the Earth with his blood; not on all seven levels at first. Rather, the energy from his blood trickled down to every level. In that way, he saved all humanity on Earth by shedding his blood upon the cross.

At first, neither they, nor we, understood how powerful the mind of Lucifer was becoming, that he was influencing us even without our realizing it. He was doing our thinking for us. We had to learn this truth the hard way.

Seeds of intelligence had already been planted in the minds of souls by the Source of All Being and the Great Father. As minds opened, humankind began to look differently at others. A most noticeable aspect of this transformation from spirit to physical instantiation was hunger for love. This attraction made humans eminently curious as they began to notice differences between males and females.

Adam and Eve existed among them. Eve knew she was to bear another being because the world needed to be populated to accomplish the divine plan. With this in mind, she tempted Adam.

Lucifer and Mother Nature Are Both Mired in Anger

Mother Nature cried out to the Heavenly Father about the arrival of humanity and said, "This cannot be!"

The Heavenly Father, in his wisdom and love, placed a loving energy over the Earth and replied, "They are a part of you as they are a part of me. Care for them and love them. When it is time for them to return to me, I will give them my love to spread upon the Earth."

Lucifer was "tied" at first to only a very small portion of Earth. He did not surround it. He experiences the loss of the Heavenly Father over and over again. It is already a form of judgment against him. He could not move or be heard. We do not know how long it lasted. There was no opportunity during that time for him to cause any harm. The power of sin was what freed him from that spot to begin to influence Earth with his reign of terror.

Lucifer surrounds the Earth, but he cannot enter it or any of the other planets. Distance is not a problem for him, only the closing of our hearts, minds, and souls to him. Planets once pristine are now out of balance and rhythm because of his intervention. The entire universe is harmed in various degrees by his actions.

It seems Lucifer is telling Mother Nature he can do whatever he wants with whoever he wants. It does not matter to him how much she loves the animals she has created. Besides, Mother Nature is angry at human beings for destroying her beautiful creation and is very upset at how much the animals she designed have changed. More and more, she is acting like Lucifer, though this craving and immersion in blood will never be as successful as they imagine.

Fittingly, considering their spiritual monozygotic origin, there is a lot of him in her. So much so, she does not realize she is doing exactly what Lucifer is doing when she unleashes destruction upon the Earth. In anger, she will further this destruction. Together, they will cause plagues with the potential of wiping out large segments of life on Earth.

Her disregard for humanity is legion. She does not believe there is anything special about human beings, nor does she harbor any hope in humanity's ability to discern right from wrong. In her view, only she and Lucifer are special, and only when they are together: a fulfillment that will never happen. She is not close to the other pairs of archangels, namely Jesus/Mary and/or Marguerita/Jacobin. She felt close to the Heavenly Father when they were creating Earth together, but that was long ago. She has since slowly drifted away from Him.

Mother Nature was very angry when she saw what was happening to what she and other supernatural entities had created. A terrible storm shook the Earth; revealing that what was happening on Earth was contrary to the divine plan. With anger shared with Lucifer, she caused great floods and violent storms, thus creating severe problems for man and animal. Thunder from Lucifer and Mother Nature came next. It expressed an anger never possessed before.

Earth was still beautiful, but no longer vibrant. Earth began to shake, and water lapped over it for the first time. Although still in spiritual form, humans felt fear as well as a desire for power. The animals sensed what was happening. Some sought comfort and protection, even friendship from the human spirits, until they saw the anger surrounding them.

In the midst of this developing cataclysm, humankind realized the necessity of finding caves or of building shelters to provide protection from Mother Nature's punishments. This terrible storm was followed happily by a beautiful harmonic sound produced from spiritual energy. It was Marguerita's voice penetrating the entire Earth. The rain ensuing from Marguerita's intervention wiped away some of the evil that was beginning to take hold across the planet.

Mother Nature wants nothing more than for Lucifer to return to heaven, where she might be able to rule together with him. At the very least, she would love to reign on Earth with Lucifer. But it will never happen. The Heavenly Father will not allow it. Neither will the higher beings, especially Marguerita, because it is not in the divine plan. It would endow too much power for the two of them to manage.

Mother Nature does not realize Lucifer is responsible for the spread and development of so much destructive evil on Earth, including what she has cocreated. If she had a choice, she would destroy the human race. She would start all over again, giving the two of them another chance to achieve their megalomaniac aspirations. Fortunately, for humanity, Marguerita will never allow that to happen. It was a blessing Lucifer and Mother Nature separated at the beginning of their lives.

Many times, Mother Nature has begged for her and Lucifer to come together, but he has always steadfastly wanted to be alone. As much as they had been joined together at birth, and though she still loves him, it remains impossible for them to join together. Marguerita will not allow that to happen, even though she is their mother. They would become too strong. Marguerita stops her from joining Lucifer on Earth. Mother Nature can only project herself to him. Lucifer will only approach her if he believes he can steal some of her energy to become even stronger.

Plan of the Heavenly Father for Lucifer

The Heavenly Father did everything he could to prepare us to live with Lucifer, but fact is, he should never have given us to him. It did not make Lucifer happy, nor was it a place where we would ever be fully safe. Many spiritual forces can cloud our minds in determining what is right and wrong. A tiny bit of truth can enlighten us in ways we cannot imagine. A guardian angel can reveal it.

According to the divine plan, it was not time for the trinitarian (i.e., three-in-one), self-sustaining relationship found in the triangles of life throughout the universe. Lucifer gave his full attention to the Heavenly Father and became a part of Him. Lucifer believed he was created to be one with the Heavenly Father, and not only to sustain Him.

Driven by love for everyone, the Heavenly Father also seemed to want to be one with Lucifer. He believed Lucifer to be an anonymous wonderful gift to him. He did not know who this entity was or from whom or where he had come. Regardless, He loved him completely.

No matter what he has been doing, Lucifer must eventually rest. When he does so, he gives fallen angels the freedom to select whatever evil they wish to instigate. When Lucifer awakens, he resumes complete control. The fallen angels then scatter everywhere to see whatever evil they can find or cause.

To stop people praying is one of their first priorities. It is also Lucifer's. They try to get those already doing evil to do even worse things. They are motivated by their anger at what they believe the

Heavenly Father has done to Lucifer and to them. It gives them a kind of euphoric high.

The fallen angels did not know the full truth about Lucifer before they joined his rebellion. They are aware now that when he burns himself out, he must rest. That weakness never happened in the heavens and, only recently, on Earth. Archangels who exerted control while Lucifer rested suddenly find themselves attacked and under relentless assault when he awakens.

They crouch down like frightened children, unwilling to even look into his eyes. They know he does not want anyone to think they are higher or greater than him. Each time this happens, they become more tired and worn. They cannot do as much for him as they did previously. The energy they are gathering is tainted more and more by sin.

From his first moment on Earth, Lucifer craved to return to heaven. He wanted to force the Heavenly Father to come to Earth and exchange places with him. An evil mind can give birth to strange ideas when it is filled with hatred. He only "loves" the Heavenly Father for his power. Jealousy will never allow him to stop trying. He has evil purposes in mind.

One of them is the delight he takes in showing the Heavenly Father how happy his children were once on Earth, but no longer. He knows this will cause the Heavenly Father to "shut down" or be worried about His children. It is completely antithetical to what the Heavenly Father desires. Consequently, Lucifer shows him evil on Earth as often as possible. It is as if he is trying to prove he has nothing to do with it, that it is rather the fault of "free will." His strategy is to open the Heavenly Father's mind to the effects of evil. He also wants to make evil look good. He is still trying to do so.

The Great Father's ultimate goal was to allow man the use of free will to rebel against Lucifer. Since Earth was the domain of the Heavenly Father, the Great Father was powerless to initiate or force humankind's rebellion against Lucifer. The hope was that humans, endowed with multiple aspects of sensory input and the power to reason, would better understand what was happening on Earth and who specifically was responsible for this devolution. Equipped with this knowledge, the hope was that humanity would use free will to turn away from Lucifer and recommit to the Heavenly Father.

Being cut from heaven and sent to this mysterious place made Lucifer very angry. Upon his arrival here, he did not notice the incredible colors of the planet. These colors were so strong and brilliant that it was difficult to breathe. When Lucifer became extremely angry, he developed what we now know is the smell of sulfur. It is one of his distinguishing characteristics. Fallen angels are attracted to it. With advanced instruments in the future, humanity will be able to locate the material vortexes where fallen angels have resided since they followed Lucifer to Earth.

Good angels also have a cycle within them. It informs them when it is time to rest and be renewed. A cycle within the fallen angels reminds them of their need to return to Lucifer for energy.

Lucifer did not understand his part in the story of creation before he set out on his quest to replace the Heavenly Father. Knowing the divine plan now does not seem to have lessened his desire, even as he is fighting for his existence. He knows that our understanding of the divine plan is limited, and that the divine plan seems subject to change. We are spiritual beings who have taken on a physical body because of Lucifer. He wanted this to happen because when we were spirits, we did not pay enough attention to him.

There is a significant difference between higher beings and us. We receive a glimpse of what our next life will be before we are born. We choose that life while in the heavens. We can select only one life at a time.

Theirs is one continuous existence throughout the universe from birth to final judgment, all without "death." It was not that way for Jesus/Mary or Marguerita/Jacobin. They have each spent different amounts of time on Earth as human beings; they have experienced mortal "death."

Lucifer always had enough sense not to extract too much energy from souls returning from their reunion with the Heavenly Father. Lucifer acted surreptitiously and, with cunning, not wanting his degenerate actions to be noticed.

When Lucifer becomes angry, he burns up some of the energy he took from the Heavenly Father. He is never pleased or satisfied, no matter what the fallen angels have done for him. The result is that he loses more energy than he is receiving. This is good for us.

Marguerita's First Experience as Human

Since the beginning of life on Earth, Lucifer's most bitter adversaries have sought to limit his influence on the Heavenly Father's children entrusted to him. These adversaries—our loving supporters—are his mother, Marguerita, and his brother, Jacobin. They have remained hidden from him. When they arrived in the first bag of seeds, she looked for a place where she could hide her spiritual presence.

Marguerita chose to hide in a bush, with rose-like flowers, an overpowering smell, and many thorns. It kept others at a distance, even after they had developed a physical form. All those who had come in the twelve groupings of human souls given to Lucifer ate flesh, except Marguerita and Jacobin. When we do evil and take life from one another, we make it easier for Lucifer to drain energy from us, thus weakening our free will. All were affected by Lucifer when they came to Earth.

Rosary beads symbolize the energy that will bind Lucifer after Marguerita makes him hear all he has done. The cord or rope is, in actuality, an energy force with which he will bind himself to her in an effort to obtain her energy. The obverse will be the case: it is she who will be binding him. It will not be instantaneous and will, in fact, take a long while. Things will get so bad for Lucifer that he will not be able to stand the sound of his victims' cries. Ironically, he will find comfort in his mother, Marguerita, even while being bound and constrained.

Jacobin was always with Marguerita, but not seen. Lucifer was very angry with Marguerita and sought out her beloved Jacobin to attack and upset her. Lucifer came close to the human spirits but did not touch them. He did not see Marguerita in the bush and did not know Jacobin was within her, despite being drawn to it. He was attracted to it, glided closer, and said, "You shall be condemned as I have been. I know not who you are, but I will make your life on Earth miserable." He knew an entity was part of the bush. He did not realize it was his mother.

Lucifer and Jacobin have been separated for so long they can look at and not recognize one another, even as they are attached in some way as brothers. This is still true today. Marguerita continued to hide Jacobin when they came to Earth together. This gave Jacobin more time to evolve.

The rain and thunder were caused by Lucifer and Mother Nature together. She both received and took energy from him. She was angry now because the animals she had created possessed an energy called blood. She did not like the fact that the spiritual world was changing. Lucifer felt just the opposite. It is what he wanted.

In anger, he called forth fallen angels from their earthly vortexes to spread his evil. Once he opens them, they are opened until the end of time. The Earth became very, very dark. It was a resting period for all of creation for the first time. Anger caused Lucifer to rest. There was only natural light from Earth's elements until the Great Father created the sun. That is why we have night and day. Darkness reminds us how evil entered Earth.

The Great Father is concerned about Lucifer, but He has not been in contact with him despite being his father. The Great Father is tempted to try talking to him, stopping him from doing his trademark evil. He knows that by talking with him, Lucifer could actually abscond with some of His energy during their discussion. Above all, He does not want to interfere. It is difficult for Him to watch what His son is doing. Marguerita is prepared to give Lucifer tough love, even though she is his mother.

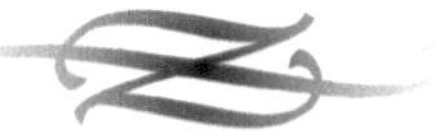

Lucifer Creates Evil on Earth

Evil is like a virus, although difficult to describe. Evil can spread rapidly through the universe. Lucifer has created the conditions necessary for it to flourish. The heavens do not seem to be able to stop this virus without our prayers. We tend to take for granted—or totally ignore—the power of prayer. Lucifer does not want us to use this blessing from God. It is important to pray so the positive entities of the universe know we want them on our side.

Lucifer spreads his evil like a virus all over Earth. He uses humanity as a vehicle for evil to show how powerful he is to the Heavenly Father. He wants us to think he will be able to return to the Heavenly Father. A part of him surmises it will never happen, but the strong desire remains. It is a desire that will never end until his power is cut by Michael the Archangel, the transformed Jacobin.

When Lucifer awakened, the rose bush was no longer there, but the smell of the beautiful flowers remained. Lucifer became so angry that he did something he had never done. He called upon Mother Nature, even though they did not like one another. When she came to him, she tried to coerce him into finding out who was in the bush. He explained he could only ascertain it was a human soul.

From that time until now, he has traveled all around Earth, surrounding it with his evil destructive energy. It can be said that he touches everywhere filled will anger, hatred, and distrust. His burning insides make him appear black, red, and orange on the outside. He actually has something of the appearance of an archangel but is not as brilliant as he once was.

Lucifer can sometimes project himself as the beautiful archangel he once was. He only does it when he wants to call forth fallen angels scattered around the world, urging them to cause ever more destruction, pain, and suffering. Every time he does this, the demons call out to him, "We need more energy."

His response is, "Find it. I have given you enough. Take the bad energy. It will make you feel fulfilled." He has not revealed to them that he has little to no communication with the Heavenly Father. He does not talk to them in ways they understand.

He is angry because Marguerita has taken away much of his strength and provides only enough for him to continue. Consequently, he must rest to regain strength. He is akin to a candle in the night, though not yet ready to burn out.

The Heavenly Father firmly believed Lucifer would learn from the wrong he had done, apologize for it, and therefore be allowed to return to Him. Essentially, a prodigal son storyline. As a pledge of belief in Lucifer, the Heavenly Father entrusted His human children to Lucifer and asked him to care for them. He hoped Lucifer would teach them many lessons, especially right from wrong, but life on Earth began to turn evil, resulting from the gift of free will from the Heavenly Father to Lucifer's subjects.

The energy of the Heavenly Father was declining. As a result, human spirits returning to Him to be renewed were changing because of it. They were no longer the same beautiful spirits they once were, in large part, because of how their relationship with animals was devolving. At some point, animals began to turn on human spirits, albeit purely in self-defense.

After his arrival on Earth, Lucifer—in a state of rage—threatened, "My dear humans, I will destroy all God has made: humans, angels, animals, and the land itself. I will pit man against man because I have the ability to read and influence what is in your hearts and minds. I am the son of a God. I knew human beings would disobey the Heavenly Father from the beginning. They will do so until the end." Lucifer will never stop trying to mislead the Heavenly Father, hoping he can return to heaven. He lusts for it.

Atlantis

Established by the Heavenly Father for His love for His children, Atlantis was the name of the first of twelve earthly centers of learning. The first group of human souls seeded on Earth were the most intelligent because they had also been the first group gifted to the Heavenly Father as His children by Marguerita, the Great Father, and the four Brothers. They were also endowed with the most creative and powerful energies. Such was their esteem and prominence, they accompanied Marguerita and Jacobin in that first group given to Lucifer.

A special angel was created by the Heavenly Father to convince a very large group of human souls, who had been with Him from the very beginning, to live with Lucifer in a new and strange environment. He intended to energize them through a twelve-step process of physical and spiritual development on Earth to become even more beautiful, to become more like Lucifer who had become more like him. It was to be a very long process, one far beyond their or our comprehension.

Wanting to help the Heavenly Father, the Brothers also tried to inspire God's children to honor and give glory to the Heavenly Father, just as the Brothers' subjects rendered unto them. The Brothers took interest in humanity from its developmental spiritual beginning through the six stages or levels of learning within the Earth. Many gifts would be given to humanity, gifts necessary to lead good lives on Earth. Lucifer, however, was already planning on how to destroy them. His only desire was to return to heaven to continue his maniacal quest for power. He wanted to be ruler of the known universe.

As a result, each successive group of souls received lesser gifts as Lucifer gradually depleted the Heavenly Father's life force. The

Heavenly Father gave these souls to Lucifer so that he would teach them right from wrong as a consequence of His gift of free will. He fully expected Lucifer to return to Him with these children. Free will allowed them to do that.

Each group of souls remained together through each of the twelve steps of learning. The first group never wanted to leave the Heavenly Father because they loved Him so much. They resembled Lucifer in their deep desire to return to the Heavenly Father, most notably at the moment of separation, albeit motivated by entirely different reasons in their heart and soul.

Successive steps of growth were designed to inspire the greatest amount of learning. Each group was supposed to remain where they had been sent until the prescribed time. Only then would an angel, created by the Heavenly Father, tell them where to go next. Lucifer had other ideas in his attempt to distort this learning process. It was a blessing, however, that he could not go where they had gone, even though he had been given great power and influence over them in the Heavenly Father's desire that His children be properly cared for.

Lucifer cleverly tempted them to go volitionally wherever they desired to go in the learning process. He wanted them to think for themselves because only then could they be influenced by his great powers. He believed Earth had been given to him as supreme authority. And therefore he could do whatever he wanted with anything or anyone on it. He firmly believes that even today. Marguerita has firmly closed the gates of heaven to him, but he also believes the Heavenly Father will take him back, not realizing (because of his diminished powers) that Lucifer wants to destroy Him. Neither the Heavenly Father nor Lucifer were aware of the existence of other beings in the universe. Neither have we until recently.

The first group to visit Atlantis truly loved the Heavenly Father. They set about using their minds to find a way to return to Him. Their desire had nothing to do with how they felt about Lucifer at that time. It was simply that they loved the Heavenly Father so much, missed being in His presence, and longed for the fullness of peace flowing from His love.

Process of Learning

Each of the twelve learning centers had been given its own name. The human souls were willing to move from center to center, completing the full cycle more than once, because they believed it might provide them with a way to return to the Heavenly Father. We do not know the length of this process; but in our concept of time, it might have been millions, or even billions, of years. We still play an intimate role in this journey.

Structures built within each of these centers will be uncovered in the future. They had brilliant minds that fostered self-idolization. They began to ponder how similar they were to the Heavenly Father. Lucifer constantly reminded them of that. He also began to foster division among them, thrilled at the friction he instilled. He could read their minds, injecting thoughts and ideas and urging them to accomplish his nefarious purposes.

Lucifer was aware of—and especially concerned—about this first group because he knew many wonderful and powerful gifts had been granted unto them. He assured them repeatedly there was a way to return to the Heavenly Father after completing their education. They would not have to die to achieve this reunion, even as he knew he was promulgating a falsehood. Stated succinctly, Lucifer was jealous of them because they might be able to return to the Heavenly Father without him. He only buttressed their heavenly return to increase division among and within them.

At that time, it was not necessary to return to the Heavenly Father to be renewed as it is now because sin did not yet exist. Lucifer provided them with some energy, but it was already tainted from what he had done in heaven and the anger he now felt for them. That anger was eating away at him. He began to change, no longer as beautiful as he once was. He wanted to believe the Heavenly Father would call him back to heaven because the Heavenly Father needed his help. His only intention was to put the Heavenly Father back to sleep again. He bragged, "I'll show Him my strength."

Lucifer gave the inhabitants of Atlantis only as much energy as was needed to change them. And it did change them. They began to fight openly with one another like never before. They began to doubt rather than trust one another. Their understanding of free will became distorted.

As a result of their development after a very long period of time, physical bodies grew over their spiritual essence while still maintaining the ability to create things seemingly out of nothing. One such creation was a kind of spiritual ladder to return to the Heavenly Father. Lucifer was, however, always trying to distort and confuse their thinking because he did not want them to reach the Heavenly Father before him.

Human beings became dissatisfied with their spiritual existence when Lucifer's incessant temptations convinced them animals possessed greater abilities than they: a manifestation of interspecies jealousy. Humans eventually got what they desired. The more frightening aspect is that Lucifer actually got what he wanted. He wanted these spirits to become physical because only then would he be able to control them fully. He did not have that level of influence over them as spirits. All of creation was suddenly at war with itself. Lucifer was willing to break every rule to make life as evil as possible.

Eventually, Lucifer's temptations and false promises convinced man he could attain the abilities of animals by eating them. Humankind did so with gusto. When carnivorous behavior was no longer enough to satisfy mankind's cravings, Lucifer convinced humankind the divine goodness experienced in other human beings could be obtained by consuming their flesh, i.e., the advent of cannibalism.

Lucifer was well aware of this demonic progression. He is most pleased by what he has initiated and witnessed. Still, as much as he aspires, he cannot become all controlling. For example, he cannot invade the Brothers' planets any more than he can reenter heaven because Marguerita has permanently shut the gates to him. His only recourse is to try to influence them externally just as he does to human beings on Earth.

What Happened to Atlantis

Some on Atlantis prayed constantly, looking intently for a way to leave it. They did not know that other life existed but felt the need to escape Lucifer's negative influence over their lives. They could not stand the anger and division, even though they were still communicating telepathically. When the island of Atlantis began to rumble, a vibration affecting the entire universe, they knew it was time to leave, but they did not know where to go.

Many engaged in self-worship, marveling at what they were able to accomplish. They devolved into three distinct and different groups of people where once there was only one. Each occupied its own select world. Lucifer would have liked to destroy all of them right then and there in front of the Heavenly Father and then direct blame onto themselves. He wanted to demonstrate his power but had become too weak to fully deal with the upheaval.

Then, without warning, the Earth shook so violently that it was knocked off its axis. Some of the inhabitants escaped by means of a modern ship they had built earlier. They landed on the second learning center where, to their surprise, there were other human beings. Though different from one another, all could communicate telepathically. Some began to condemn the Heavenly Father for this rupture; others blamed socially engineered experiments for what was happening.

Ultimately, a great explosion, akin to a super volcano, erupted beneath Atlantis, sinking it deep into the ocean floor. The structures they built still exist. Someday it will be discovered. It was Lucifer who caused the destruction.

All worshipped the Heavenly Father in the beginning. Lucifer never liked it because he wanted their full attention. He wanted to be their god to demonstrate to the Heavenly Father the great power he possessed to rule over the Earth. He used humankind's creations against them, always making it look like an accident. He did not want anyone to become powerful enough to take his place in heaven.

We carry some of this knowledge in our minds throughout many lifetimes, but it is not always revealed. It depends on how our mind works and what we are to accomplish in that particular life. Those who died on Atlantis went back to the Heavenly Father. That is still another reason why Lucifer hates us. All human life must eventually return, whereas Lucifer can never return.

Some of the souls who died on Atlantis have returned to Earth. They arrive with great knowledge which, by the granting of free will, can be used for either good or evil. Jesus chose one person from each of these twelve learning centers as His apostles.

How Did We Get Here?

The process of transubstantiation from purely spiritual to combined spiritual/physical incarnation occurred in seven distinct phases. Each of these phases was related directly to the seven strata with which the Heavenly Father created Earth. These equate with the seven times the Great Father unknowingly gave Lucifer transformative energy.

Each phase was distinct and possessed a unique energy designed to improve the development of these newly-created spiritual beings. The more you learned, the greater your responsibility became. Lucifer had power to influence what would happen on these levels, but his mind was blinded to what was happening.

Lucifer did not know about this process of preparation or that he would eventually be charged with caring for souls. He became furious at only becoming aware of the process after his banishment. He believed he should have been consulted. In his mind, he thought he knew more than anyone else, including the Heavenly Father. Crusades and wars begin when he gets angry.

The timetable for all created life is written in the pyramids and myriad other historic places located throughout the Earth. Sites hidden all over the world to protect truths are cared for by an angel assigned to each site.

Because his mind had been blanked, Lucifer is only now becoming aware of the importance of these locations. They contain truths not known by humanity. Only advanced technology will find them, though it will be difficult to decipher them. When discovered, they will reveal and confirm there are four phases to life: each phase consisting of four periods. Each of these phases lasting millions, possibly billions, of years.

The first phase encompassed the evolution of spiritual beings into physical creatures. This transformation came about because of the false promises of Lucifer. The second phase is characterized primarily by development of cerebral intelligence in the physical human, essentially how we perceive ourselves today.

In the third phase, humanity began expressing itself creatively, perceiving the precious quality of life, developing existential understanding, distinguishing between right and wrong, embracing individual maturation in accord with the divine plan. That third phase ended in 2020. The fourth and final phase has now begun.

This fourth phase is marked by greater enlightenment, an enlightenment preceding the final judgment and the end of time. This should not be construed negatively, though, because we must always remember the soul is a sharing in the life of God and, therefore, can never be terminated. All our lives are recorded in our soul. The Heavenly Father has given us many chances to live as we should, not just this one life. He is a loving God. The Spirit within Him may be our judge.

Summary

At the very beginning of human existence, Lucifer was jealous of the ability of human souls to return to the Heavenly Father for renewal of His pure-loving energy. Lucifer could not take any of that love or paternal caring away from them. Lucifer's jealousy "infected" human souls because the way back to the Heavenly Father was eternally closed to him. We do not know how long it took, but Lucifer was able to impose a curse on the human race. The effect of his jealousy introduced sin into God's creation.

On each level, your mind became much more engaged, though Lucifer was still able to project as a beautiful angel even while gestating evil intent. Marguerita only allowed him to do that so she could eventually show him his true depraved self at the Last Judgment.

Sin, therefore, took form when human beings became vulnerable to Lucifer. Through a series of nefarious acts, Lucifer has successfully influenced man's exercise of his free will and reversed the evolution of man as God originally intended. Lucifer led us to believe we were moving forward after influencing us to go backward.

There is, therefore, much negativity on Earth. Many people have turned against the Heavenly Father, our one true God. It was not unexpected in the heavens that this would happen, and that man would or could become greedy. They saw Lucifer as a brightly shining angel and then at what he has become since. They think he is as powerful as ever. In some sense, that is true. He has been able to impress those he has carefully selected as accomplices to help him on Earth. He has attained for them much of what they have wanted from this worldly life.

The fallen angels who followed Lucifer to Earth continue to appeal to our free will to lead us into sin. When you experience this power of sin for the first time, there is something attractive about it; it is not easy to control. It wants to influence and dominate you. When Lucifer's mark turns from red to black, it exudes a "glow." The red makes you feel comfortable, but in a strange and mysterious way, the black elicits evil thoughts, allowing them to surface in our consciousness.

This evil has continued to spread and cause more harm than we ever imagined. More and more people seem to be listening to Lucifer than to the Heavenly Father. The impact and effects from evil will remain until the Last Judgment, despite the fact that many good souls are currently entering Earth to fight against them. Many of these souls lived during the time of Christ and possess special gifts to unite us in this struggle.

PART 2

The Great Awakening

Truths Discovered

Our time on this planet has now entered a new and final phase. One of the most critical times for humanity has just begun. Millions of years may pass before time ends, and we are finally judged. Regardless, the beginning of the final period of these four phases of earthly existence started recently. Life is now changing rapidly, especially our understanding of its history and development.

The emphasis during this period is focused on the revelation of truths to be discovered, embraced, and implemented. If we are ever to achieve the eternal peace and joy for which God created us, we must embrace and incorporate the meaning and purpose of these revelations.

It is a time of awakening, a time for revealing many hidden mysteries. These revelations are owing to humankind's increasing ability to understand the heart and mind of God. It is a time to decide what to believe and how to live. This urgency is heightened as humanity becomes ever more attracted and committed to evil rather than good; bluntly, as humanity becomes more attracted to Lucifer than to the Heavenly Father. Fiction, not truth, is the map many people have chosen to follow. They have been blindfolded by evil. This evil must now be exposed.

When the Heavenly Father ultimately gave the human souls to Lucifer after their development on the lower six levels of Earth had been completed over the course of millions of years, He said to him, "I give to you, my son, this planet and all those within it. Fear not, for you will be like a god to them, much like I am. You will give them knowledge and direction. I have given you a great gift. These are the ones you will care for. They will listen to you."

The Heavenly Father wanted Lucifer to know and accept that humanity exists as His children, not Lucifer's. No thought was given to the possibility of humans not returning to the Heavenly Father. No consideration was given to the possibility we would exercise our free will to follow Lucifer's way of living, rather than the Heavenly Father's directives. The Heavenly Father weeps for us in the midst of so much evil, disease, and bloodshed because there is little the Heavenly Father can do to stop it. He seems to believe now he should not have given the gift of free will to both us and Lucifer.

Lucifer instilled on Earth evil ways he had learned through the misuse of his power in the heavens. He did it with the assistance of archangels who followed him to Earth. These archangels could not leave the vortexes deep within the surface of Earth until called forth initially by Lucifer. He did so only after devising a plan to sustain his power and authority. This became necessary because he could not take, nor was he receiving, as much energy from the Heavenly Father as he had before being expelled from heaven. Now, he craved ever greater power, believing the archangels could obtain it for him by taking it from humans—just as he had stolen it from the Heavenly Father.

The archangels believed he was a very beautiful and powerful being. As a result, they were prepared to do whatever he wanted. He told them convincingly they were special, and he was going to give them even greater power.

When he first sent the fallen archangels out among the human souls, humanity did not pay any attention to them. Perhaps it was because the human souls felt closer to the animals, immersed equally in the beauty of nature all around them. When the archangels returned empty-handed, Lucifer became very angry. He expected them to know what to do without him having to tell them because they had seen what he had done in heaven. Lucifer failed to understand these archangels had just come out of their vortexes into a new world and an entirely different way of life. They were filled with great wonder at what they saw. This made Lucifer irate.

With great anger, Lucifer told them directly they must transform human souls, make them deviate from their created purpose, and become complacent, obedient subjects of Lucifer. He did this because he believed he had been given this new world and, therefore, could do whatever he wanted with it. The Great Father—who was Lucifer's "father"—understood what Lucifer's intentions were but could do nothing to stop him.

When man began to aspire to do what angels could do, the Angel of Light went to the Heavenly Father and said, "Father, you have created Earth and placed both humans and angels on it. The humans seem to have become very dissatisfied. What is to become of them?"

The Heavenly Father's energy seemed to decline before he said, "I have no tears to shed, but I do feel sorrow because I am able to see what will happen. I cannot understand how Lucifer has changed from being so strong and from being my favorite."

Suddenly, there was a terrible sound like a crash. Mother Nature broke in and said, "And what has he done to me? He ignored me because he thought I was not good enough for him."

The Heavenly Father answered, "It was not your role to be with him. I gave the Earth to him, not you."

Mother Nature felt intense anger and demanded to know, "Then I am nothing?"

The Heavenly Father exclaimed, "No! You are still special in my eyes. You will create new and special gifts for the Earth."

While all this was happening, Marguerita and Jacobin were hidden together among the first group of human souls sent to Earth. They looked and acted like everyone else. There was no way to identify them. If Lucifer had known and been able to do something about it, life would have evolved differently.

The Heavenly Father was protecting Lucifer. Marguerita was protecting Jacobin. It was all in accord with the divine plan, though it may seem to have been wrong or ill-advised according to our present knowledge and wisdom. We fail to realize things are not always what they appear to be.

Lucifer provided energy, along with very specific instructions, in unleashing four archangels among humankind. They were to tease and torment humanity. Lucifer asked if they wished to fly, to do all the things animals were capable of doing. This was the first instance of archangels and humans communicating with one another.

The animals could sense what they were discussing, as did Mother Nature. She helped create animals and became "frightened" by this possibility. She hoped nothing evil would happen but gave a special gift to the animals before anything could happen. She made them stronger and faster without truly knowing how these gifts might affect the animals. At first, the humans did not want to harm the animals, desiring only to absorb enough energy to become like them.

This change in the divine plan helped the animal's intellect expand more readily. The human mind developed more slowly out of jealousy toward the animals. Human consciousness remained focused on exploring myriad developmental potentialities. This is precisely when Lucifer was able to enter and influence the human mind.

Unknowingly, the archangels had prepared the way for Lucifer to accomplish this mission with the energy he had given them. He did not care how much energy archangels gave to humans, but he was careful not to dilute too much of his own. His plan was to pit humans and animals against one another as a way of convincing the Heavenly Father of His failure.

The minds of animals evolved faster because of the type and amount of energy Mother Nature used in their creation. Animals were Mother Nature's favorites, not humans. She created them as companions to Lucifer, a veritable gift to her brother.

Mother Nature is very upset at how animals are used by "warped minds" who believe what they are doing is good. They do not understand, as has already been demonstrated from the past, how evil spreads from experimenting on these divine gifts. It is frightening and disappointing that we have not learned from our own mistakes.

Evil was growing stronger and spreading farther. Humankind became ever more motivated to take whatever it so desired from animals as compensation for what Lucifer's angels were taking from humans. They believed there must be nothing wrong in doing to humans what Lucifer was doing to them. They simply wanted to share in animal capabilities. What they didn't appreciate was Lucifer's ability to manipulate their thinking.

Being able to read minds provides better opportunity to change them. Lucifer is extremely capable of this. He received this ability from the energy he took from the Heavenly Father—energy used to respond to our human needs, even before we pray to him. Great harm is caused when truth is distorted and not fully understood. One of Lucifer's weapons is to make us doubt God's love as well as questioning our own goodness because of the wrong we have done.

At first, the humans and animals did not pay much attention to Lucifer. They did perceive a slight connection to Lucifer but were unaware he no longer had a full, loving, nurturing connection to the Heavenly Father. Human souls did not suspect Lucifer yearned to return to the heavens for the express purpose of overwhelming the Heavenly Father, ruling the universe in His stead. When humans returned to Earth from the Heavenly Father, first as spirits and then in physical instantiation, Lucifer could only take a portion of the energy they had received.

Of all the animals inhabiting the Earth, only the snake showed respect toward Lucifer. Though they shared many secrets with him, they were not respected in return. By revealing these secrets, the snake caused ever greater evil in the world. It is appropriate Virgin Mary will crush the head of a serpent when she takes her place on Earth after the death of Marguerita.

Human Life as an Experiment

Humankind altered its development when it began to covet animals. Man sinned when he began to eat the flesh of an animal, even more so the flesh of his own kind. This avarice arose from the jealousy inflicted on them by Lucifer because he was unable to go back and forth to the Heavenly Father for renewal the way humanity could. We now can right that wrong, albeit conscious that such change can be very painful.

As humans evolved into physical beings, they became more animallike. No longer could they stand erect. Instead, they were bent over like many of the animals. Their arms and legs moved differently. Fur grew around them to cover the nakedness of what they thought was their spiritual body. Human beings were covered with so much fur, it was difficult to tell male and female apart. Humans began to experience hunger for the first time, an expanded palate drawn to different tastes. Their souls, however, remained different from the souls of animals.

In the near future, some people will become convinced their blood will strengthen when mixed with animal blood; that it will prolong their lives. Human beings will begin to think like animals, craving certain foods enjoyed by them. Three different kinds of animal blood will be mixed with human blood in hopes of attaining better results. Some people will even start to believe blood will make them younger. They will be misled by false promises. Chemicals will also be added to make this blood even more appealing.

We will return to a time when vicious tribes lusted for blood, believing such infusions would make them stronger. They sacrificed human beings to obtain it, believing they were able to overcome death by doing so and with the help of their false gods. They covered their bodies with it. Lucifer places these sick ideas in human minds as a way of making them feel creative.

The excitement of shedding blood has grown strong among the fallen angels. They experience exaltation in watching others kill, be it human or animal death. They believe they are exempt from punishment for the evil they have caused. Fact is, none of us are exempted. Ultimately, there will be an end to this evil. An accounting of its atrocious deeds will be made.

Lucifer distorts truth by convincing people the shedding of blood pleases God. Like Lucifer, fallen archangels are excited by the sight of blood, especially from an innocent baby or child. These archangels take energy from this innocent blood and spread it over the Earth. That is why there are so many violent murders and abortions.

It excites the fallen angels even when people donate blood. It is like a drug to them. It excites them even more when someone receives blood from another person. They extract energy from blood wherever and whenever they can find it. In time, we will be able to drain blood from an animal, cleanse it, and incorporate it without changing it for use in human beings.

It has been said that "What goes around comes around." Many of those who caused destruction by shedding the blood of others will shed their blood in a future life. They will choose to do this to better understand evil and its many effects. They may hope to change the way they lived, but not all will be successful. When you enter a new life, you do not always listen to your heart, mind, or soul. You return again and again to repeat the same evil.

This is ironic because blood brings oxygen and nutrients to all the parts of the body as necessary sustenance. Blood also carries carbon dioxide and other waste materials to the lungs, kidneys, and digestive system to be removed from the body. Blood fights infection and carries hormones around the body. Our circulatory system, therefore, can be seen as the physical embodiment of God's loving energy and paternal guidance for us.

Struggle to Exist

Humans realized they had to go in search of food to satisfy hunger. What had come naturally, spiritual sustenance, no longer existed. Mother Nature had provided food, such as berries and seeds in spiritual form, but humanity could no longer pull necessary life-sustaining energy from the Earth. What we see today in material form, they saw in spiritual form. Food was as real to them then as it is to us now.

At some point, animals began to turn on humans but did so in the spirit of self-defense. The Heavenly Father was very unhappy with this unforeseen development and tried to stop this spreading of evil. When souls returned to him for renewal, he gave them ever greater amounts of loving energy so they could return to why they were created in the first place. He opened their minds so they could experience life as it had originally been created, with no desire for blood or the sickly obsession with death.

The seeds of human life are souls. Each is unique. Even as we gestate in the womb, we have the ability to think, understand, and feel the soon-to-be reality of human incarnation. We have been created that way. We know where we came from, what we will become, and how we should live our lives. At our first breath, however, we forget it all. Life becomes a blank page; it's what the British philosopher, John Locke, called the *tabula rasa*. Everything we knew intrinsically is suddenly forgotten. We are placed on a new path with the freedom to author our own life choices.

The archangels possess the ability to know what each soul possessed from previous lives, which souls were weaker and, therefore, more easily manipulated. The archangels did not have to speak directly to them. They emitted a sound like a vibration that fascinated human beings. It garnered enough of their attention to convince them animals were their enemies, not their friends.

The animals knew what the archangels were doing was wrong. If humans truly aspired to become like them, such jealousy could be very harmful. They could sense and feel the negative energy. When the animals realized this, some fled into the waters or other parts of the Earth. There, they remain. They are beginning to reappear now. They have not evolved much, some not at all, since this exodus. Not wanting to be harmed by what they feared was about to happen, some human beings also fled. They knew in their hearts what was happening was wrong. Humans and animals subsequently went to one of the many different levels within the Earth.

Despite her great wisdom, Marguerita, even with Jacobin's help, could not save them all. Those she could not save she urged to flee because her power was not as strong as it had been in the heavens. Neither Lucifer nor the archangels knew what she was doing because she was so well hidden. Lucifer did not realize how many souls were being freed. Those who fled have not developed like man in either mind or body.

Over millions of years or longer, man and animal began to develop a physical side to their spiritual being. There was still love between them, albeit expressed telepathically. Humans remembered how the archangels had promised, "You shall be like the animals in the ways you desire and develop." Although they did not fully understand what that meant, they knew it was contrary to what the Heavenly Father wanted. They knew Lucifer was placing them on a path to evil and destruction. He did not want man to be only spiritual because he was afraid human beings might become more intelligent than him.

After a long period of time, the knowledge of a spiritual body seemed to be removed from man's mind. Humans were attracted to one another, but there was no real caring or love between them. They did not have emotions but continued to evolve physically. Like an animal, they walked close to the ground. They ate animal flesh but did not know why its blood excited them. Once Lucifer recognized they could kill, he was pleased. This opened the way for him to take another step in his devious plan. Shedding blood was a very important part of it.

Man began to kill one another for the energy they believed would give them greater power. In the process, they lost their love for one another and even killed their own children. Animals also changed. They stopped communicating not only with man, but also with their own species.

It bothered Lucifer when humans began to cook flesh. He wanted their faces and bodies to be covered with blood because he could then protest to the Heavenly Father and Mother Nature, "Look at what they are doing. See what you have created?" When the Heavenly Father heard him, His energy waned, and He began to slow down. This thrilled Lucifer. He wanted to believe the Heavenly Father would lose all His energy, thus allowing him to take control of the heavens. Also, when the Heavenly Father responded to his taunting, Lucifer was able to draw more energy from Him.

In the beginning, human beings had more than one mate. It caused many genetic problems. They would even propagate with their own children, believing there was nothing wrong. They had little understanding of what it meant to bring life into the world. Every disease goes back to this time. Lucifer knew there would be problems, but he chose not to intervene. He wanted many children to be born, desiring to abscond with the energy he could take from them. He had no love for any of them. Sadly, the Heavenly Father could not stop it because He gave Lucifer power over the Earth.

There was no such thing as a family unit. Children began to develop all kinds of problems because mothers had no love for their children. Animals were also given the ability to procreate at the same time as man, but they had more care for their offspring. When a human being had a child, the mother just left it there. The child meant nothing to her.

Mother Nature cried out to the Heavenly Father and said, "This cannot be!"

In His wisdom and love, the Heavenly Father placed a source of loving energy on the Earth and replied, "They are a part of you as they are a part of me. Care for them and love them. When it is time for them to return to me, I will give them my love to spread upon the Earth."

Lucifer grew very angry because he believed he should have been given this energy. In response, he placed in the minds of humans a desire to fight and kill one another. A bad situation became even worse because human beings were willing to kill their own children or someone else's child. Seeing what was happening, animals began to kill man to protect themselves. They also began to eat their own.

Lucifer Today

Lucifer has been going through a transition. Because of the evil he has caused on Earth, he is not receiving enough life-sustaining energy. As a result, his energy is becoming paper thin with what appears to be holes in it. His eyes have also become like red coals. He understands what he has done. He has only one chance to release those souls kept in bondage by the fallen angels who watched over them in what has been called purgatory, but he will not do so. The good news is that another will do it.

Lucifer has not achieved everything he wanted. He has been unable to stop our guardian angel and our angel of death from carrying us back to the Heavenly Father to be renewed. This is what Lucifer desired most. He does not want us to have what he cannot have. Lucifer is growing angrier and more jealous of human souls. As a result, he is getting less and less life-sustaining energy from humans because of what he has personally done to mankind. It is akin to a poetic justice.

Lucifer grows angry when Marguerita reveals what we see as truths, but he views as secrets. He is afraid of truth, especially those about him. He is the ultimate source for the spread of deadly viruses. The fallen angels help to spread them with the assistance of others who have given their lives to Lucifer. Viruses develop from the blood shed on Earth and from all sin. It deepens our commitment to evil.

From far above the Earth, you can see red or hot spots where much blood has been shed. Some spots are bloodier than others. You can tell where the first blood was shed and then in succession from the varying shades. Our era has been the worst period because of world wars and many other conflicts. More blood has been shed on Earth than we can begin to imagine. These spots glow and make Lucifer very happy.

Marguerita is constantly guided by these spots because there are more souls in purgatory than on Earth. Some have been good; others have been bad. All have experienced the anger and fear Lucifer instilled in them. Still, others are unaware of why they are there. So much hatred has been spread in the world since man's first sin of killing an animal to eat its heart.

A band of angels always accompanies Marguerita, an indication of how difficult it is to come face-to-face with Lucifer even when you are his mother. She will do anything for human beings to experience the love of the Heavenly Father. When necessary, we are called to come face-to-face with evil so the love of God will prevail. In some cases, we will fail; in others, we will succeed. Regardless the anticipated result, we must try.

There is a burning anger in Lucifer as he tries to track down Marguerita during her earthly sojourns. He should realize by now that hatred and anger chip away at one's spiritual being, but he does not. The spiritual barrier around him cannot be repaired. It is a reminder of how much love the Heavenly Father had for him and, at the same time, a reminder of how much evil Lucifer has done.

Lucifer does not think time is running out for him or for those on Earth. He believes his kingdom will never end. In the meantime, Marguerita continues to release souls who have been bound in purgatory. The fallen angels are not concerned about them one way or another. There are always new souls to replace them. These fallen angels do not realize the wrong they are doing, nor the good they could do.

If we did not know better, we might believe there are times when the Heavenly Father appears to love Lucifer more than He does us. And while it may seem contrary to human reasoning, keeping Lucifer in control on Earth is a way of preventing even worse events from happening. We must not forget Lucifer is part of the Heavenly Father whose love for Lucifer transcends any one reason. We must not presume to know these reasons as they are not easily detectable. They may, in fact, come as a surprise.

Pure love is the most powerful energy in every universe. It is what protected Lucifer. Now that some of it has been lost, the fallen angels see him different. They cry out to the Heavenly Father, "We followed him, but we were misled. How will we be judged? Will there be no mercy? Why should we do his bidding?" They fail to recognize that Lucifer will not be their judge. Lucifer has become weaker, though he believes he can regain his original strength if only he can become one with Marguerita or Jacobin.

There is still a thirst in the world to kill, a thirst motivated by the false belief such killing makes one powerful. Our guardian angels speak to us through the mind, trying to stop us on those occasions, but we do not always listen.

To change the direction human life was taking, the Great Father gave women the capability to restore life to its original divine attributes. The female side of creation embodies those ontological attributes endowed, experienced, and enjoyed before Lucifer's demonic influence.

The human body evolved for the purpose of propagation of the species. The ability to procreate developed when Mother Nature believed Lucifer deserved to have many more followers in his kingdom.

Spiritual beings in the heavens, however, hoped additional human beings could influence Lucifer to stop the evil he was doing—fostering in him a love for the children given to him, but for whom he had no respect. He considered himself to be far superior to them in every way, but he grew worse by living contrary to the divine plan. For her part, Mother Nature gave both humans and animals similar internal organs, all of which were designed by a higher spiritual being. She hoped awareness of this similarity would bring them closer together. Sadly, it has not.

Purgatory

Love is the foundation of life. A world of perfection is a world of love. God wanted a world of perfection to develop within a world of love, where perfect spiritual beings could live. Such a state of being must be in perfect balance to complete the full development of man, angels, and animals as intended by God. In the creation of Earth, it was not. Furthermore, a most significant question to be asked is: Why did God give us free will?

The gift of free will is so much part of human ontology that it remains with us even as we transition between death, the reflective hiatus prior to renewal, and one's rebirth into another human life. Truth be told, we have decisions to make upon our death. That is when fallen angels seek to influence, connive, and convince us not to return to the Heavenly Father.

Under Lucifer's direction and sharing somewhat in his power, fallen angels can convince souls immediately upon death, not to return to heaven and be renewed. They try to influence and subvert the gift of free will endowed within us by the Heavenly Father. As a result, we can choose to return to Him or not return to Him.

When we pass from this world, we are free to decide whether or not to enter heaven. In heaven, we review in detail this recent past incarnation in preparation for another earthy existence. This next existence is meant to further the soul's learning and the acquisition of divine wisdom. Lucifer, however, never ceases trying to influence us, especially at that pivotal moment, to live our next life in ways benefitting his selfish desire to become supreme ruler of Earth.

Forlorn souls have languished in a purgatorial state far longer than we can imagine. They have no physical bodies, nor do they experience emotions. They reside in a lonesome solitude, never communicating with one another. Every so often, the fallen angels who watch over them emit a sound evoking the assertion, "Don't be frightened. Don't leave." It is repeated over and over.

At the end of a life, Lucifer and his fallen angels try to convince us we should remain alone in this realm called purgatory, i.e., a state of spiritual imprisonment. They spew a negative energy force over those souls. It keeps them essentially comatose, preventing them from thinking about the sins haunting them and keeping them away from repentance and cleansing. We do not fully know why, but the evil binding them limits the number of opportunities to be released to three. These are souls for whom we must pray. Only the guardian angel who has been with them since their birth and their angel of death can release them from this spiritual imprisonment. But this requires acquiescence by Lucifer and his fallen angels.

This guardian angel remains with the person to whom it has been appointed from the very beginning of its existence until final judgment. It includes those human beings who have undergone experiments on other planets. Guardian angels give greater care to those who suffered excruciating physical and mental pain. Those victims seem more aware of their guardian angel's presence than we who enjoy good health.

At first, these souls listen to Lucifer and his angels. They remind them of what consequences they might suffer because of their past sins. Lucifer exclaims, "They are mine!" and places a kind of spiritual "glue" over them. When Marguerita's golden light flows over them, their hearts are open to the Heavenly Father's love. Their minds attune to the truth Marguerita brings. She urges them, "Go to the light, or you will be lost. There is only so much time." She knows they were trapped by fear of the unknown, lost in time, and feeling unworthy of forgiveness.

This enrages Lucifer, making his eyes burn like hot embers. Marguerita fears not. She is surrounded by protecting angels and feels the love of these angels, even if she cannot always see them. We should feel the same way about our guardian angel. Marguerita wants to expose all of Lucifer's tricks. One is how he led poor souls to believe he was the one who actually loved them.

The next step is vastly important for souls. They must make a definitive freewill decision about what they want to do. It can be difficult for our guardian angel to inspire us to do what is right. They show us the good and the bad and try to influence us in ways we do not even realize.

When souls choose the Heavenly Father, an energy force paralyzes the demons, nullifying their ability to intercede. They are left paralyzed and catatonic. In their stead, a good angel filled with golden light shows the poor souls how their sins can be cleansed and forgiven.

Pain and suffering remain when they leave, especially from places like concentration camps. Their energy is restored so they can break free from their spiritual bonds. They can lift themselves up to freedom because the fallen angels overlooking them are blinded by Marguerita's divine light, thus severing the fallen angel's communication with that soul. No longer will they awaken to hear the words: "Stay here. Do not leave."

The released spirits look alike, but each soul is unique. There are subtle differences, often slight and unseen, very much like human DNA. Some are grateful for having been released, even if not yet ready to return to the Heavenly Father. Many are walking on Earth among us. Human beings and spirits cannot see each other.

When released from corporeal bondage, souls are supposed to say, "Take me to the Father's home." It is time now for all who have been released by Marguerita to return to the Heavenly Father. Most have been frightened and imprisoned by Lucifer and the fallen angels for far too long.

There are some who do not want to come back to this world, no matter the cost. Life is a mystery, as is the good and evil within it. Lucifer has been surrounded by a band of angels who have insulated him from hearing the cries of those whom he has harmed. This spiritual barrier has begun to break. He began to hear the evil he has caused. Until now he has heard almost silence. Some of those cries between periods of rest have come from those who have not been able to cross over to heaven.

Millions, maybe even billions, of angels who chose to follow Lucifer to Earth were selected to approach human beings at the moment of death to convince them not to enter heaven. The most powerful and effective weapon they use is fear. It is one of the greatest enemies of love.

They wield enough power in those circumstances to convince us that great pain and suffering await us in heaven because of the wrong we have done in our last life. They want us to believe God is waiting to punish us. Without our life forces being renewed, we gradually fall into a semblance of deep sleep, a state where even our own guardian angel and angel of death cannot communicate with us.

Lucifer does not want us to pray for these poor souls. He is very angry at the great success his mother, Marguerita, has had traveling in spirit form throughout the entire Earth, convincing souls to return to their heavenly home. When Lucifer sees her golden light shining in parts of the world where souls are calling out to be freed, he sends more fallen angels to remind them they are more than poor souls—they are instead lost souls for which there is no hope of redemption and rebirth.

We have free will, but sins like pornography can leave a stain burned into our brain. This sin is very difficult to erase spiritually as it continues to excite us across incarnations. This euphoric feeling can remain in the brain even after a soul has been cleansed. Like a deadly virus, it waits to be released again. We do not know for what purpose, but perhaps this residual evil energy may be needed and released for Lucifer's final battle with his brother, Saint Michael the Archangel.

To gain their freedom, poor souls in purgatory need the powerful intersession and loving energy from our prayers. Prayer is critically important. It can accomplish greater good than humans realize. We would truly pray more often if we only knew just how great a gift it is. The whole world is in need of prayer and blessing.

When we pray, the loving energy we ultimately receive from the Heavenly Father remains with us through every life, no matter how we have lived. The Heavenly Father never gives up on us. He is a divine source of hope; whereby, each revelation of truth weakens Lucifer.

Prayer helps to open the minds of confined souls to the fact that we humans possess free will. Free will was granted—and is to remain sacrosanct—until the final judgment. It can be limited depending on how we choose to use it. Our free will can never be taken from us completely. Free will has the power to reduce Lucifer's influence. That is why Lucifer cannot force himself on us without our being complicit.

The freedom to do good also bestows the freedom to do evil. Consequently, we must invite Lucifer into our lives and nourish him continually with evil. It allows him to invade our thoughts by promising achievements of deleterious and demented fantasies involving worldly society and flesh. In believing his many false promises, we inevitably draw closer to him. Truthfully, because of the advent of sin, engaging in evil acts offers us more immediate gratification than doing what is right, good, and just.

Consequently, we need to show our love for the Heavenly Father via heartfelt prayer. Full truth reveals the Heavenly Father's actions were always motivated by great love for His children. For humanity, however, this truth and goodness are not always apparent.

Lucifer still receives a small amount of energy from the Heavenly Father. He also has squirreled away other energies that should never have been given to him by the Source of All Being. He hopes to gain advantage in his relationship with the Heavenly Father, poaching energy from vulnerable souls passing from this life to another. Humankind's many life iterations and temptations means there is no longer any pure energy to be taken from adults. That is why Lucifer urges people to kill babies and children.

When Marguerita comes to Earth, she is protected by a kind of energy cocoon surrounding her. Lucifer can see her but cannot touch her. He desires this energy because he has never seen anything like it. With this energy, Marguerita is able to help others wallowing in the deepest oceans or the highest mountains—places human beings have never been.

Many souls in purgatory have been saved by Marguerita. Salvation means being reunited with the Heavenly Father. Despite being shackled by the power of Lucifer, many will return to Earth to do great things. They will become stronger because they have felt God's power of love. We are given only so much time and so many lives on Earth.

Despite All, There Is Hope

There is a great deal of negativity on Earth. Many people have turned against our God, i.e., the Heavenly Father. Truthfully, it was not unexpected in the heavens that humanity's rebellion would happen; that man would become greedy and self-centered. The celestial realm recognized Lucifer as a bright shining angel but also see what he has since become. They perceive him still as being powerful. In some sense, that remains accurate. Lucifer has been able to continue impressing those carefully selected to help him on Earth. He has attained for them much of what they have wanted from life.

Our world is being polluted in so many ways by sin. The fallen angels still abscond with energy for Lucifer without realizing the harm they are doing, even to themselves. Humans possess free will and can say no to the evil they are doing, thereby preventing energy from being unknowingly provided to Lucifer. We are learning so much more about how drugs (legal and illegal) can alter our brain and, perhaps, even our soul.

Everything has a time, even learning about the power of sin and truth. Sin can block truth, but human pain and suffering can cleanse any blockage established by Lucifer. He does not want the truth about him to be revealed. He has only so much energy to prevent it from happening before he has to rest and receive an energy infusion from the fallen angels.

We can take solace from the fact that the fallen angels are slowly rebelling against Lucifer. Some have begun to talk back to him, even refusing to do what he wants. This infuriates him and causes him to burn out. He is forced to rest much longer.

A portion of the energy fallen angels had collected for Lucifer was taken and stored on another planet. It is more negative than positive. The fallen angels are being asked if they want to continue serving Lucifer. They would have been very strong and capable of destroying everything if they had been able to keep that energy.

This energy was not destroyed but will be given back to the now fallen angels at the end of time. It is saving grace these fallen angels will be spared rather than condemned forever when this age concludes. Post-apocalypse, some of these fallen angels will join with Lucifer, orbiting where planet Earth used to be. The majority will want to return to the Heavenly Father but even if this wish were granted, they will not be as close to Him as they were before. They will have great insight when this energy is returned to them, enabling them to make informed, enlightened decisions.

This eternal struggle is akin to a two-edged sword. Jesus gives energy to the Heavenly Father who then passes it on to Lucifer. This is what keeps Lucifer alive until the prescribed end-times. There are good reasons why the Heavenly Father wants to keep Lucifer alive. While Lucifer thinks he is gaining additional strength, this energy is affecting his mind. Soon, fallen angels will not be as obedient to him as they had been. It is the Heavenly Father's way of holding on to Lucifer—trying to control him while at the same time trying to safeguard His human children.

We need to understand the Heavenly Father better. Why does He not answer when we cry out to Him—giving rise to bitterness, sadness, anger, and resentment? We are told again and again that He has given us free will. Consequently, He cannot always help us even as we cry out to Him. He loves us deeply no matter what happens. We should—we must—live with hope. The answers to questions like this will be given to us at the very end of life.

Jesus came to cleanse our hearts and souls and instruct our minds. In doing so, He precludes the need for any human blood to be spilled. He shed His blood on the cross to cleanse both us and the Earth. His blood in death has become the blood of life for salvation. The energy from His blood on the cross trickled down to every level (though not all seven levels at first), thereby saving the Earth—even as He continues to sustain and renew the Heavenly Father with His energy and strength. It is in this loving energy that the Heavenly Father now rests.

Through His suffering and death, Jesus left His blood on Earth. Doing so allows Mary to come back again and again to continue sharing His love with us. We should not forget Mary. Remember, she also left some of her blood on Earth while giving birth to Jesus. In that regard, Mary marked Earth even before Jesus.

There is a mark within our soul that will activate when Marguerita dies. Marian apparitions will comfort people in this world filled with great turmoil. Despite all the evil perpetrated from the far distant past until today, throughout future centuries, we can—and should—live with hope as we endure the struggle between good and evil.

Lucifer does not have blood like us. He has an energy force, but he cannot use it to mark Earth and claim it as his own. When Earth was verbally given to him, he believed that meant it was his alone, that he could do whatever he wanted with it. He was wrong.

What is happening now may be a sign Earth is being readied for a being who will claim to be a god. He is hidden now, waiting until the prescribed hour. Mary gave birth to Jesus. Marguerita and Jacobin have John Andrew. Lucifer and Mother Nature have given life to this child, who is not human. He is the one we refer to as the Antichrist. His appearance will initiate an even greater battle between the forces of life and death, of goodness and evil.

There may be as many as four Antichrists in the world at one time. Each will try to outperform the other three, seeking to prove he is most powerful. Many problems on Earth will emerge as it spits up huge flames and dangerous toxins. The removal of coal and other minerals placed in various places in Earth will allow this to happen.

The son of Lucifer and Mother Nature will touch the hearts and minds of the masses. They will worship him and give him honor and glory. A handful of people from all over Earth will know he is not what he claims to be. Few will listen to them because their ears will no longer know what is true and what is not. Lucifer will become very jealous of his son. He is the only one who can harm him, proclaiming, "I have destroyed. I have destroyed."

Still More Hope

The Earth has begun to reveal many of its secrets. These discoveries will keep Lucifer wondering and pondering why it is happening. He believes the Earth is his, not realizing it was only loaned to him in the hope he would change his ways and return to the Heavenly Father. That has not happened and never will. The Heavenly Father is always waiting for us to come back to Him to be renewed.

There are many additional items currently lost and housed in the Vatican. These items will be found. They will reveal knowledge, information, and secrets the church and other spiritual centers did not realize they had. Likewise, many jars found in and out of water in caves will contain truths.

In many ancient communities, they wrote how evil permeated among them. They hid these truths in various places in the earth so they would be found in the future. One jar from antiquity speaks of two who will come to reveal truths capable of disrupting the faith of Christians. Other jars will reveal more about the lives of Jesus, Mary, and Peter, and what will happen in the end-times. There will also be a map of life from Marguerita in one of her incarnations.

Those who walked with Jesus will return once again to open the gates of light hidden from the human race. Life has many mysteries. Divine words will reveal them, along with all the twists and turns created by Lucifer. They will reveal what he has lost and become.

All the apostles are returning to life at this time. They live—or will reside—in different parts of the world and will follow various religions. During this period, the magnetic attraction of the rock given by Jesus to Peter will radiate throughout the world, drawing these reincarnated apostles here to Pittsburgh. They feel Pittsburgh is a blessed part of the Earth. It is akin to the Wise Men following the bright star to the site of the Lord's birth.

Humanity is introducing much evil into the world via its desire for power, a motivation inspired by Lucifer as he seeks control until the end of time. He hates Christian churches. The crux of the issue is that some of the church's teaching comes from man and not from God. That makes it earthly dogma rather than divine pronouncement.

Some church fathers believed humankind would seek perfection in this lifetime if they believed and accepted that we only had this one life to live. They believed human beings were not as intelligent as in fact they are. Scholars who proposed or thought differently were sometimes put to death. The church became very corrupt because of Lucifer. The church will crumble, and many people will leave it. In time, they will return when the church changes some of its ways. New life will result.

It is the only way the church can be cleansed. Despite the church's challenges, reception of Holy Communion is the greatest gift anyone can receive in this troubled world. We do not receive it often enough. Fortunately, God will nourish and guide His church.

Those who followed Christ were chosen originally by the Great Father. They do not know this. They were old souls who had overcome much. They laid close to Marguerita and Jacobin and were protected. Many of them could not write but had scribes.

Mary had much compassion and love in her heart for humanity and will come back to be with us. On her death bed, she said: "I will not abandon my children, just as my son has not." Many who lived on Earth will be coming back at the prescribed time to help and encourage human beings.

Efforts have been made to bring animals and human beings closer together since the beginning of time. This quest continues today. Many of the results are surprising. This effort will see greater success as animals and human beings begin to better understand one another.

God, in His infinite wisdom, is always inviting us to open our hearts, minds, and souls to a deeper understanding of truth. The hope is that we will recognize just how precious the gift of life is. In understanding ourselves better, we can appreciate our relationship with God more fully.

Toward the end of all life, man will begin once again to communicate through the mind, just as he did in the beginning. As God intended.

The way Lucifer used the energy given to him by the Heavenly Father, together with the energy he stole, created greater evil and destruction. It has had a very deleterious effect on all the planets. We can expect the forces of evil to continue working against us. These forces believe they, alone, have the truth.

All life is awakening and is achieving consciousness. Life must first reach the potential for which it was created before everything is destroyed at the last judgment. The celestial entity, Him, the overseer of all creation, has started this process through the Golden Light. The Brothers are providing additional energy to accomplish this, even as they justify human experiments as bettering humankind. They, in turn, are also activating their own planets.

Lucifer wants to convince the Brothers, especially Brother 4, that they should side with his efforts, influencing people to foment greater evil. People will turn against Lucifer when they realize what he is trying to do.

A sound heard throughout the universe will announce this great awakening; its echo reverberating back to Earth. Humans who had been experimented on will return to their original creation. The energy that changed them will remain on the planets to which they were sent until all is destroyed at the end of time.

When Lucifer hears and feels his scream, he will say to his mother, "Look at what I am suffering." She will respond, "Come, and I will protect you," but she will bind him to herself, and there will be peace on Earth for a while.

Life is truly a mystery no one will ever understand. This truth can be either a warning or an expression of hope. We will determine which comes to fruition by whether or not we learn to live together in peace.

One of the lessons we will have learned by then is that knowledge, wisdom, and truth are precious gifts that should be shared throughout the universe. Each and every one of us can do something important in the struggle against evil. It is difficult not to repeat what you did in previous lives, be it good or bad, because of Lucifer marking you when you first came to Earth. Nevertheless, we still have free will. Strength of mind is different in everyone. In your last life, you usually do something very, very good or very, very bad.

Truth has the power to guide and turn us away from Lucifer in this final period of time. We must know to whom it is leading us. The most important moment for humanity, and it is only a moment, is when we will be judged whether or not we are worthy to receive God's love forever.

There is so much mystery in life that has not yet been revealed; but in the near future, we should anticipate enlightenment.

PART 3

Kindred Life in the Universe

Life on Other Planets

When humanity begins to travel into deep space, it may or may not find the planets inhabited by these unfortunate souls. If we did happen upon them, there is risk we could unintentionally kill them with the viruses we unwittingly carry—like the scourge early European explorers, either knowingly or unknowingly, visited upon the native populations of America.

The first phase of spiritual conception occurred when the energy of love from The One, the ultimate source, the greatest power in creation, created a group of five higher spiritual beings in the universe. We might term these supernatural entities as extensions of His being, but they are not gods, nor are to be considered as gods. Each of The One's spiritual extensions was given distinct responsibilities as well as the power and authority needed to accomplish creation of this new universe. These are the celestial entities named the Great Father, Him, the Source of all Being, the Supreme Being, and the Golden Light. A celestial genealogy is detailed in *The Story of Creation*.

Each Brother was created by the combined energy of Marguerita and The Great Father. The Brothers were created and subsequently appointed to oversee designated subjects in a very complex, difficult to understand universe. The Brothers and their subjects reside in energy rings surrounding each sibling's individual planet. They are entirely spiritual entities.

The Brothers remain on their particular planet. They never come to Earth. It is their subjects who have visited Earth. Some of them inadvertently return home with a virus-like energy picked up during their earthly visitation. This is causing very serious problems to exist now throughout the universe. Perhaps even in other universes, but more on that later.

Unlike our Heavenly Father, these four Brothers and their followers were not given angels to personally assist them, nor were angels granted to any of their kingdoms. When, eons later, human beings were created, the Brothers and their subjects began to wonder why the inhabitants of Earth had angels, but they did not. Thinking themselves more developed and powerful than Earth's inhabitants, they also wanted to know why they could not propagate the way humans were capable of doing.

The four Brothers each possess a similar mark or "soul," but each exudes a distinct spectral shade of the color purple, thereby marking this uniqueness. The Brothers were discrete and separate entities at first but have since learned about one another's existence, including how to work together. This is because changes are happening rapidly throughout the universe.

Each Brother rules his planet with the assistance of three subjects. These subjects are literal extensions of his being. Each Brother selects one subject from each of his planet's three surrounding rings. These three subjects assist the Brothers, but in truth, they were never intimately connected to the Brothers. Being revealed now is that these subjects were not a genuine extension of the Brothers' being, unlike the case with much of The One's celestial hierarchy.

It is imperative to keep in mind that Lucifer is the ultimate source of evil in the universe. After influencing human beings to do wrong, Lucifer is now tempting the Brothers to do what they can to selfishly make life better for themselves. It is the same way he tempts us.

The Brothers once tried to replicate human life on Earth but failed. Their fraternal representatives wanted to travel to Earth to discover what was happening on this relatively new planet. The Brothers claim they did not know their followers were going and, in fact, did not want them to go. Yet they did nothing to prevent this exploratory incursion, motivated by their belief that Earth was a perfect world in the process of devolving into evil. The Brothers were concerned about how their planets might be affected; a concern—and trick—instilled by Lucifer.

Considering these shared origins, it is imperative we understand (and accept) that these aliens are in truth familial relations to us. They are akin to what humanity understands as "cousins."

To refresh and clarify: a cousin is the son or daughter of an uncle or aunt. The word "cousin" also refers to one related by descent in a diverging line from a known common ancestor, as from one's grandparent or from one's father's or mother's sister or brother, a kinsman or kinswoman, but relatives, nonetheless. This notion is further supported by the fact that reported alien encounters feature sentient beings similar, though not identical, to humans in their metabiological composition. We share in one another's energy or life forces.

This reasoning was explained in Charles Cockell's book, *The Equations of Life: How Physics Shapes Evolution*. Cockell, a professor of astrobiology at the University of Edinburgh in Scotland, contends there is a "universal biology." Alien adaptations, significantly resembling terrestrial life—from humanoids to hummingbirds—may have emerged on billions of worlds. Now these might be the result of "evolutions," or they may very well be part of The One's desire to create creatures possessing unique ontological attributes.

These entities could sense and feel the energy of others flowing around them. This is because energy from all life is connected. Our energy is like a string to our Heavenly Father. Life-giving energy spheres envelope each of the Brothers' planets and is what sustains the Brothers, allowing them to communicate through energy discharged by each.

This is very much in keeping with recent postulations related to String theory. String theory postulates that the fundamental constituents of the universe are one-dimensional "strings," rather than point-like particles. The vibrations of these string-like entities determine the particles' properties. For example, mass and charge. String theory also requires six or seven extra dimensions of space and contains ways of relating large extra dimensions to small ones. String theory advances a literal connection between all matter and reinforces the familial connection between these celestial entities.

Gift of Free Will

At one time, humans were the only created beings who possessed free will; but when free will was given to humans, it overflowed into the rest of the universe, albeit in a slightly different form. Other more highly developed created beings inhabiting other worlds were jealous of this gift. They sought to obtain this gift in any way they could, thus fundamentally altering its meaning. It gave the Brothers the opportunity and freedom to conduct experiments on human beings.

The unfortunate complications this has caused (problems we are about to expose and examine in-depth) is what keeps the four Brothers together in an unfolding search for unity—seeking the good their uninvited intervention was supposed to achieve. When the Heavenly Father gave us free will, He expected we would always choose what was right and just. The same mandate should have applied to the Brothers.

Amazingly, the Brothers were unaware of the Heavenly Father's existence until long after they had been inspired to help Earth deal with the developing problems they observed. They could not understand why or how human beings, who were placed on Earth as spirits, developed into physical forms. They were baffled by the temerity of humans killing the very animals that had been created to show human beings how to love. Then, incredulously, humans began to kill one another. What the Brothers believed to be a blessed existence on virginal planet Earth became transformed into a place of evil. They feared the same might happen to them. These developments on Earth were beyond the scope of the Brothers' understanding as they do not think like we do, finding it very difficult to comprehend the actions of humanity.

The original visitations to Earth were spurred on by the belief and perception that Earth was a planet inhabited by created beings who needed help. It was as if they believed a divine spirit sanctioned these actions, up to and including visitation, and subsequent experimentation. This was at odds with the innate perception of their own governing rules and ethos. These rules forbade such intrusion and intervention.

The result of this severe dichotomy is their admittance (finally) that they were wrong to experiment on human beings. There will not be any deliberation at the final judgment. There is a consciousness that all in our universe will honestly judge ourselves and that judgment will be confirmed.

The followers of the Brothers were invisible when they first traveled to Earth. They had the ability, though, to project themselves into physical form. This was a capability they had learned to do much earlier in their evolution, though forbidden now by their own code of behavior.

Occupants of the first energy sphere around Brother 1 came to Earth with a limited number of subjects. They have since claimed that they only wanted to teach and inspire us. The inhabitants of Earth at that time had not developed vocal cords. So the two groups communicated telepathically. Sadly, humans are no longer able to do so as they have lost many such higher abilities as a result of sin, plus humanity's transition from spirit form to physical manifestation.

Him, the Golden Light, the Source of All Being, and the Supreme Being all contributed different energy to assist in this effort. When each of the Brothers independently saw the experimentation taking place by their subjects, they wanted to stop it, but now claimed they could not. They wanted us to know they do not want their involvement—and responsibility—to be known because of what has been and is being revealed. They would like to hide the truth, blaming those on Earth for all the problems in the universe resulting from humanity's freewill choices.

There are different sacred rules for life, wherever it has been created and according to its level of development. These rules were implanted in the minds of the four Brothers and then imparted to those assisting them at the time of their creation. They, alone, possess this knowledge and wisdom. A similar set of rules, what we know as the Ten Commandments, was given later to the fifth Brother, our Heavenly Father, for the Earth.

Desire for Power

The first four Brothers had been watching our development as spiritual beings on Earth from the very beginning. At first, they felt sorry for us and tried to help. They felt driven to ask three questions as humans began to change significantly: 1) Why were humans able to procreate and they could not; 2) why do humans have angels and they do not; and 3) why do humans kill one another?

As a result of Lucifer's constant input, the Brothers concluded initially that humans had absolutely no worth. Lucifer insisted we were no different than the most primeval creatures, similar to the bugs they saw on Earth. Still, the Brothers wanted to understand why we were killing and eating both animals and human beings. That is when they decided to experiment on us, motivated by the desire to find out why this was happening. Truth be told, they are still conducting these experiments today—even though they deny it.

It makes one wonder, as a species, why those who are more highly developed always believe they know better while continuing to do evil. As a result of their actions, some followers of the four Brothers have brought untold pain and suffering to their four planets. Those who have been allowed to return from experiments on Earth are carrying back a destructive virus generated from the sin caused by Lucifer on Earth. This virus has spread over the entire universe, causing great suffering for the inhabitants of these myriad worlds.

Lucifer convinced the Brothers that experimentation on humans would be in their self-interest. The first purpose of this experimentation was to be able to deconstruct, and then recreate, a human being. Again, the incentive behind this was the Brothers' bewilderment at the human ability to procreate. They perceived humans to be inferior life-forms. How then could humans procreate while they—believing themselves to be a superior species—did not have that capability? They held to the belief they too should have this gift or power. Consequently, in defiance of rules clearly known to the Brothers, many human beings have been abducted from Earth expressly for procreation experimentation purposes.

When blood began to soak Earth from a lack of respect for life, two of the chosen leaders from each of the four planets were sent to Earth. They were to help us with whatever they thought we needed. By doing this, they believed they could mark Earth with their energy and claim it as their own. Unknown to human beings, they had already begun to conduct experiments on them. Some were completed on Earth while others were performed on their own planets with abducted human beings.

Some of the Brothers' followers undertook more experiments than others. From these experiments, many different forms of life were created. Some were returned to Earth and some to other planets (of which we will discuss in greater depth shortly), but the majority were not. For example, the creature known as Bigfoot is the result of Brother 1's experiments; Big Bird is from Brother 2; Brother 3 created the Little People; while Brother 4 is responsible for those whose height was shrunken.

Not surprisingly, the motivation for these well-intentioned but ultimately nefarious actions can be traced back to the influence of Earth's designated ruler: Lucifer. A prime example of his evil bearing can be traced to the second-in-command on each of the Brothers' four planets. These celestial authorities believed Lucifer to be a majestic, beautiful, and all-powerful angel. Hence their distress as they see his increasing deterioration.

They have come to understand tragically they will be judged like him at the end of time, though they refrain from admitting it. Owing to Lucifer's effect, their ability to rule their own subjects has been lessened greatly. Lucifer is angry he cannot rule them because he would enjoy impacting them the way he has impacted and manipulated the Heavenly Father's children. He also recognizes that the four Brothers, who have now banded together, have become more powerful than him.

After seeing how much evil Lucifer has done on Earth, the Brothers have no love for him. What they do not realize is that Lucifer has saturated them with a blanket of malicious energy. All they are able to perceive is the positive energy the Heavenly Father has provided him. Meanwhile, Lucifer has planted seeds of evil among the Brothers' followers. As will be revealed, this virus has been traced back to Lucifer.

Lucifer's reprehensible actions in using the very powerful energy given to him by the Heavenly Father, and then subsequently absconded ever more, has created greater evil and destruction than just on Earth. It has had a very bad effect on all the planets. The Brothers have not been able to eradicate it completely and are still trying to find a way to cleanse their planets. To prevent further damage, a ring of angels has been placed around each of their planets to protect them.

No one knows what to do about it, or if it will affect them more than it already has. With a willingness to try anything, the four Brothers who had never traveled previously, even to meet with one another, have come together to form a rapidly moving circle of creative energy to hopefully cleanse their planets. It is a process through which the Brothers will eventually become unified. It is also why Marguerita has been given permission to visit the Brothers' planets to speak with those humans who have undergone these wrongful experiments.

Testimony of Brother 1

The Brothers have tried to justify the evil Lucifer convinced them to do, most especially experimentation on animals and human beings. Brother 1, who is the most powerful and intelligent, likes humanity the least. In fact, he believed at one time that our planet and species should be eradicated.

He explained, "We tried to help you, but we have not received appreciation for what we have done. Yes, I gave my permission to conduct experiments on your people, but we also wanted to direct and enlighten you. Many of my subjects appeared godlike so as to enable them to rule and guide you for your own benefit. They appeared on Earth like kings and rulers.

"I realize some of them took advantage of their positions and did what they should not have done. But don't blame or criticize us until you examine what your own people have done to one another—and still do. Shall we compare what you have done to what we have done? We have seen you on Earth but have not always spoken to you. We believed at one time that our fifth brother, your Heavenly Father, should never have been created, but now we understand better from the truths that have been revealed. We also understand we must find ways to work together.

"Your planet is becoming weaker and is already beginning to disintegrate. I now understand what evil can do. Some of my subjects have contributed to it. I have to ask myself, Was I resting, or did I simply refuse to see it? Some of what I have said about you is true, but I must admit I looked upon your planet as worthless. There is so much disarray. We, four Brothers, must put our energy together to prolong life on it. Only when we begin to respect one another, and not just the planet, can there be a cleansing of all on Earth.

"It has been pointed out to me that my followers and I were not perfect. We too were seemingly nothing until we developed much further. I am beginning to better understand how the universe was created. Some of my Brothers are angry but only listen to me because I was the first created.

"I want peace and will speak to the other three so there may be more communication between us. I still do not understand you completely because a veil has been placed over my energy. Maybe it's time for me not to think I know it all. Welcome to my world."

An angel was unknowingly present, hoping to motivate him to tell the truth, albeit unsuccessfully.

Explanation of Brother 2

Other Brothers approached during this transmission. Brother 2 spoke with reverence, "I have questions. I'm not as strong as Brother 1. There was a time when we didn't know each other existed. Those around me believed your planet to be very strange, but we were willing to try to enlighten you. They went to your planet on an undetected ship. It entered your atmosphere like a ball of fire. It was a very difficult trip for them, and they had to rest for a while.

"We are not a troublesome, cruel species. There is doubt and wonderment in them, but not in me. That is why I'm sure other Brothers will want to speak to you in their own time. We Brothers are attached by bonds of energy, yet still separate. I did what I wanted by commanding those below me. They are formed in a circle that helps to keep me informed and alive.

"I have recently reviewed what we have done on your planet. We had no right to do it, but we meant well. It is not easy for me to speak to you. I believe I have reasons to question your sanity, but I must admit that my subjects have also taken animals and humans from your planet and experimented on them. They were thrilled to experiment on them to discover who and what they were and why they did what they did—especially the killing of one another.

"All four of us are different and command respect from those below us. All of us on our various planets are a part of one another. It is surprising to me that we all come, including you and your people, from the same ultimate source. I felt that I was king of the universe but realized now that I am only a part of it as are my Brothers. We have heard your criticisms many times. But you do not come off as a brilliant star gathering and sharing important information with the world.

"Yes, we too have experimented on your people and placed some of them on other planets. Some we have returned to their homes. I know now this was wrong. I have also told my subjects that it is wrong, but some of them defied me, explaining, 'Look at how they kill one another. We learn by experimenting on them.' I can't deny that what they say is true, but I feel your energy—your concern. Can we trust you and believe you will stop doing wrong? I don't believe so. I see the many problems you have on Earth. But I will respect you as I see you respect me."

The Brothers' subjects continuing experiments on our planet is alarming as is their justification that we on earth are doing the same thing to our own people. Some of their interests and actions are puzzling—and even perverted to us. For example, Brother 2 was fascinated with snakes. He liked to combine their DNA with human cells. His curiosity arose from the fact that snakes would not cause harm unless, or until, they felt threatened.

His subjects collected snakes from all over the world and inserted their DNA into various parts of human beings. They then recorded how long these human beings and snakes lived under these circumstances. The DNA of snakes was infused into the brains of human beings. As a result, these humans could no longer walk but instead slithered along the ground. Their tongues grew longer, and their skin began to change. They even shed it, molting as snakes do. Much was taken from the snake, but we do not know everything. We do know snakes no longer walk upright as they once did.

Because man was still in transition from a pure spirit to a mixture of a spiritual and physical body, it was very easy to change him. They remained whatever age they were, but their eyes changed to those of a snake. These new beings gathered in groups and no longer spoke to one another. They only hissed.

By contrast, Mother Nature did it differently when she created animals. She gave them love, knowledge, and strength. When man began to hunt animals, she gave them the ability to perceive fear and subsequently hide from humans.

Brother 4's Defense

Brother 4 is closest to us and wise to our ways since many of his subjects were placed in various regions of Earth to help us. They came mostly in spirit, not projecting a human image as Brothers 1 through 3 did. Similarly though, they were not pleased with what they discovered and observed on our planet. They saw how every inch of our planet's soil had been soaked with blood from so many wars and acts of violence.

Brother 4 explained, "I feel so near to you, to your planet, and yet so far away. I am also close to your people, but there are times when I wished I had never communicated with you because you people are killers. There is very little caring for man or animal. So I do not wish to hear the rebuke of what we have done wrong. There is going to be great upheaval with my Brothers and your Heavenly Father. Man will also revolt against man. Evil will stoke the fires of hatred, mistrust, and anger. The shedding of blood will be strong.

"We went to Earth to help you, but it was not appreciated. I understand that no one knew about us then, but nevertheless, it remains unappreciated. Of course, at this time we don't love our fifth Brother, your so-called Heavenly Father, but we have learned to respect him. I must admit, however, that I haven't seen him and don't know him. All we knew was that his family needed help, and we wanted to assist.

"If I had a heart, I would be saddened by what Lucifer has done. He turned what were many peaceful years into a living hell—as you say. It affects all of us and the entire universe. We extend peace to our fifth and last Brother for we are all interconnected."

One of his followers spoke in support of him, "I was the third-in-command on our planet. Try to understand us and not be so judgmental. As we watched you from the beginning of your world, we became aware of human vulnerability. We began to question why you changed and became so different. We wanted to find the secrets you held. How can a spirit change? How could you be so loving but then descend into cannibalism?

"We had not realized, before your creation, there were worlds other than ours, that we had siblings, and that they felt the same as we did. And so, we decided to investigate the human mind. I directed others from my world to go to Earth and find what you call 'specimens.' I wanted different humans from different ages and from different places. Yes, Lucifer knew what we were doing in his world, but he did not try to stop it. In fact, it was very strange in that he directed us to what we needed.

"As I look back now, I am surprised at how much we learned about human beings, especially how unfaithful they are to their Creator. We are the closest among our sibling worlds to you in our thought patterns. We do not eat, but we have respect for the energy that keeps us alive. We would like to be able to propagate as you do, but we see how you even eliminate some of the children you bear. We would not, and could not, kill any of our progeny.

"What we have learned has been mysterious to all of us. We too can love, hate, become angry, and have mistrust. I could tell you so much more about us, but what I want you to know is that we are not what, or how, you think we are. Yes, we were wrong [to do the experimentation], but we were somehow influenced to do what we did."

Brother 4 sees Lucifer in a better light than his Brothers, but he will not acknowledge complicity with Lucifer insofar as providing him with energy. Lucifer's scream (when he fell to Earth) awakened each of the Brothers to his presence at that precise moment. They did not fully construe what that scream meant, or initiated. It did, however, awaken among the Brothers an intense desire to commence understanding the new sentient creation called humanity.

Their first experiments were conducted solely on animals. When those experiments did not yield enough actionable knowledge, they turned to human beings, hoping to learn more. They could not touch us when humanity existed solely as spirits. Only when humans formed physical bodies were aliens able to experiment on us. At first, this experimentation focused solely on the mind—not the body. During all this, they made many mistakes; mistakes they have tried unsuccessfully to hide.

Effects of Experimentation

The technology of the four Brothers is clearly more advanced than ours. They have used it willingly, as well as their superior intelligence, in the experimentation and creation of "specimens." Now that we have discovered what they have been doing to these abducted humans and animals, each of the four Brothers would like to destroy them. Fortunately, according to their "Book of Rules" (i.e., their "Bible"), they are not allowed to kill what is not theirs.

At first, some wanted to take all the energy from our minds; others did not. Many intellects were ruined as a result of that endeavor. When they could not accomplish what they wanted to do with the mind, they turned to the physical body. Sadly, some people suffer from those defects even today. These experiments may have failed because human consciousness transcends the physical. The Brothers did not recognize the connection between mind and soul.

The followers in the first energy circles around the Brothers and their planets are becoming united in usurping control of their planets. If they succeed, they will commence making their own rules— no longer being faithful to, or willing to follow, presubscribed commandments. They do not admire, respect, or esteem Earth, despite their innate brainpower having been combined and augmented with human intelligence. As with repelling magnetic poles, this could result, unfortunately, in our potentially becoming enemies.

All the spiritual beings and corporeal creatures who have been taken from Earth are beginning to slowly awaken. When they were put to sleep after the experiments, it was a kind of death. This was so they would not remember what was done to them or who did it. It also took the physical pain away. We do not know if they had mental pain. Each is beginning to speak, and not always telepathically. It is being referred to as "The Great Awakening."

The human beings on whom the Brothers experimented have been exiled to a designated galactic region, albeit settled separately on one of four distinct planets. This is where each Brother has placed "experiments gone wrong." Until recently, they did not know each of the Brothers was performing specific experiments on human beings, nor that each Brother possessed a planet where human specimens are sent, who can no longer live with other humans.

On these planets, they live in a semi-catatonic state, surrounded by what looks like a form of Plexiglas. These poor creatures have lost the ability to speak and see. Consequently, they cannot describe what has been done to them, nor the great suffering they have endured.

Most are beginning to awaken because their planets are moving ever so slightly out of alignment. As a result, they are remembering— for the first time—what happened to them. These beings are limited to telepathic communication and then only to others possessing similar extrasensory capabilities.

Parts of their brains have been altered severely. Many of them have brains imbued with both human and animal sensibilities. The same can be said about other parts of their bodies. Still, despite the severe changes made to them, they remain fundamentally human, though it might be more accurate to describe them as part human/ part animal/part (what might be termed) "alien" or "extraterrestrial."

Some of these humans were taken from Earth when they started to develop characteristics of specific animals. They are only learning this because they were segregated from other forms of human life. None of the Brothers has ever visited them. Few of their subjects have ever shown any concern for them. Those who did were chastised.

Some look like what we refer here on Earth as "Bigfoot" and "Mothman." Others have the face of an animal; still others project finlike arms. In one process of experimentation, humans received animal parts; and animals received human parts. Sperm was taken from a male, eggs from a female, and mixed together. As these beings awaken to the changes in their structure, they have reason to be very angry. Their confusion brings them to the precipice of insanity.

Looking at one another, they experience deep emotions—emotions never felt before, most notably deep hatred against those who did this to them.

Lucifer was elated when he learned what the Brothers had done at his suggestion. He wants these "specimens" to "come home" to his kingdom because they are, after all, human beings; but they are unable to travel. He was even willing to trade one of his fallen archangels for each of them. This offer was not made out of kindness or genuine concern. Rather, he wanted control and would use them to frighten the rest of humanity.

Lucifer believed he could appeal again to the Heavenly Father by making Him aware of what was happening on Earth. It was all part of his desire to convince the Heavenly Father it was time to bring him home to heaven. There are many reasons why such an appeal will not be successful. One is that his fallen archangels are bound to Earth; second is concern among the Brothers that some of the experimented specimens might find a way to escape, become known, and embarrass the Brothers.

Both Lucifer and the Brothers knew these human extractions were wrong. Yet they continued to do them. They argued experimentation was an attempt to help humanity by bringing together what they believed to be the best attributes between animals and human. They closed their eyes, minds, and hearts to the serious harm they were causing.

The Great Father did not know this was happening. When He found out, He admonished them: "They must be released and returned home." Sadly, it did not happen. The Great Father knows He does not have the right or power to release them because these specimens come from Earth, and the Great Father is not their god. Only the Heavenly Father has that title and authority.

The experimented beings strongly desire to be returned to the Heavenly Father so they can be renewed and reborn through the natural process provided to every human soul. We do not know if that will ever happen. At present, these unfortunate specimens remain in a perpetual vegetation state. They are unable to die. They do not eat. Fortunately, they draw energy from the planet itself. The Source of All Being and the Supreme Being continually nourish them with life-sustaining energy. They simply exist at this moment without any movement.

Victim Criticizes Brothers

One of the followers of the Brothers, who chooses to remain anonymous, reveals what he has seen on the planet where he lives. "It's important for you to know there is no conception of time here. I come from Brother 1 and have watched what has been done to many human beings. We do not experience fear, nor do we possess sympathy. As I watch you from above, I can only say you are a strange lot. We don't give you names, only numbers.

"I've never communicated with a human or animal. I do not fear them and have never felt compassion toward them. I have watched them die and return. But you want to know, however, about the human beings we have altered. Trust me, we do not harm them with the energy we possess. We could, but we don't. I do not feel sorrow for those we call 'the unfortunates' just because our experiments weren't successful.

"It's hard for me to explain in your words why we did what we did. When we brought them to our planets, some were weak, and others were strong. We discovered they never remained for long in one category or another—human, animal, or like us—but instead changed slowly: each of them in a different way at a different time. Their minds never developed as we had hoped. I truly believe they should have been destroyed, i.e., 'destroy the evidence!' I've said this over and over again. When the humans understand what we have done, they will try to destroy us. But what I'm telling you is only between us.

"The unfortunates are, in our view, neither human nor animal, but a strong combination. They no longer look nor speak like humans. In fact, they are completely different from you. But in time, they will be able to communicate fully and with accuracy. They want to return to your planet, but I'm told I must not allow it because it is not time for them to go home.

"We do not experiment on our own because we're not like you. You were once in a shell before you were born. It is a shell in which I could see. There, you began to grow and develop. When you started to eat of the flesh, your bodies changed. It was an intriguing path. You grew ultimately into the form you are today. It would cause you much distress to explain the process we use to experiment on humans, a process we still do today."

[Note: additional information was then provided, perhaps from Brother 1 or one of his subjects. We have heard from still others, those willing and able to talk, concerning their own experiences, accounts different from the above.]

They recount that one can see inside the bodies of some of those on whom experiments have been performed. One is a child, undiscernible regarding its sex. He/she is among those who want to learn whether survival is possible.

The child speaks, "I was human. I was taken. It was painful. I resisted, but my body seemed to be frozen. I am unaware of time. I know I lived on Earth, but I don't know who I am. They experimented on me. I do not like the body I am in. Help me."

Some are more human, some more animal, and some more alien. It seems they are more than one person. They are strange in other ways. Some have body parts without any rhyme or reason. Their minds are connected to something giving them life, but it is slowly diminishing. They are not receiving as much nutritious energy as they once did, attributable apparently to their planets moving slightly off axis. They are now under a different influence that gives them an opportunity to tell their story, and hopefully, tell the truth.

Another human being protests, "I was one of the first to be taken. I don't know why I'm speaking these words to you. I didn't know I could speak, and that you would understand me. I know I had children. I was lost. He hurt me. Some were kind, put me to sleep, and I no longer felt pain. I don't know where I belong. I don't know who I am, but I saw your light, and I came to you. I don't know if you understand me. I know what they did, but I don't know how to explain it. My brain was scorched. Hopefully, you are here to release us? To take us home? We will give our bodies to you so that we may rest in peace."

Groups of humans were periodically taken from Earth during periods of transition or turmoil—times when they might not be missed. After experimentation, some became highly intelligent and were returned to Earth to see if, and how, they could survive. They possess brilliant minds. They are able to communicate with us because they still possess some pure energy. They exist all over the world and will reveal themselves more frequently in the near future. They want to understand us, hoping we will also understand them. Most of them, however, are fully unaware of what was done to them.

Certain victims want to protect us. They feel kinship toward us, even though some on Earth think of them as aliens. A few others would like to destroy us. These feelings were implanted as part of the experimental process. Still, they know a part of them is from the "Heavenly Father's planet." They have watched Lucifer, are aware of his strength, and would like to destroy him. They see the evil he has done, evil of which we humans have been either blind or purposely ignored. We must keep in mind that killing as a form of revenge is not permitted by divine law. Those doing wrong will be accountable to the ones doing right. No human, or Brother, will judge them.

Those who have been victimized by experimentation have traveled throughout Earth and beyond. It angers them that the Brothers will not even allow them to visit the outside orbits and atmospheres of planets where these experiments took place and where specimens reside. They protect themselves by not allowing themselves to be seen, though they can project themselves as either human or animal.

Mothman

Let us turn our attention to the sightings of what has become known as Mothman. The origins of Mothman date from November 12, 1966, when five men who were digging a grave at a cemetery near Clendenin, West Virginia, claimed to have seen a man-like figure fly low from the trees over their heads. Often identified as the first known sighting of what became known as Mothman, sightings have since been reported ranging in location from Chicago to Russia, often associated with catastrophic events.

Many are familiar with the book, *The Mothman Prophecies*, by John Keel, published in 1975. The book combined Keel's account of receiving strange phone calls with reports of mutilated pets, culminating with the December 15, 1967, collapse of the Silver Bridge across the Ohio River. The book was widely popularized as the basis of the 2002 movie of the same name starring Richard Gere.

Here is the truth about the Mothman "myth." Mothman *is* an altered human being whose modification is due to alien experimentation. This human subject was actually the first to be taken from Earth for experimentation purposes, despite others claiming to have suffered this same fate. Whether he was the sole individual taken, or part of the first group abducted, remains unclear, though alien acquisition of humans did occur both singly and in groups.

The genetic experimentation on this individual resulted in a creature possessing the wings of a bird, furry legs, the face of an animal, and claw-like hands that are attached to wings that grow from his skeletal structure. In appearance, he resembles an eagle.

Despite these gross physical mutations, Mothman's singular exceptionality is his mind. His mind is unique. While it can no longer be considered a human mind, it retains a connection to its original hominoid consciousness. To alien dismay, Mothman did not develop the way they had hoped, despite their experimentation on his brain.

Fortunately, enough humanity remains within Mothman to motivate his desire to protect us and, however possible, be like us. His heightened sensibilities have allowed him to see evil throughout Earth; he knows how deeply it can influence us, even causing problems of which we are not aware of. His heart is sad but kind. He wants to know why he was subjected to such experimentation, but all he can surmise is that his purpose now is to protect others. Humans are rightfully both frightened and in awe of him at the same time. While alien experimentation changed his physical and mental capacities, great love for the world was instilled in him when he was changed.

There are four or more different Mothman species, though they do not all possess the same designation. The third species, the one who first appeared in West Virginia, was designed for Earth alone, especially for the United States. They each return to that part of Earth from which they were taken. In totality, the Mothmen species is trying to save us from the evil spreading across the universe. They have equal power to do different things. When they rest, they are sometimes thought to be either dead or comatose, but they eventually revive.

A tiny spot on them is believed to be their soul. Each of the four species has its own leader. They are all kind and likeable, but they do not communicate with one another. Lucifer is afraid to take energy from them. He wants it only from human beings, entities whose energy or power of love mystifies him.

This individual sighted in West Virginia was brought back to Earth by a spaceship because he was more intelligent than humans. He could communicate with aliens via mental telepathy. He was even with the astronauts on their journey to the moon and may have revealed himself to them.

He attained some of the qualities of Brother 1 and some of the pure energy his followers shared with him. He feels a closeness to both man and animal in spirit because that altered part of his brain has begun to grow. Some of those who have been returned to Earth have become almost humanlike again as a result of their spiritual renewal by the Heavenly Father.

Avian Humanoids

One of the most persistent mythical images presented throughout Earth's history is that of the combined human and avian creature. Avian humanoids are common images and folkloric motifs and fictions in Greek, Roman, Manipuri, Hindu, and Persian mythology. The truth is, they are not mythologies.

There is a great deal of imagery of humans possessing birdlike wings. Examples here would include angels in all Abrahamic religions; Eris in Greek mythology and Discordia in Roman mythology; the Hindu and Buddhist birdlike creature, Garuda; the winged genies of Assyrian art; and others.

A complete combination of human and aviary features can be found historically in creatures such as the Harpies, usually perceived as bird women capable of generating tempests designed to terrorize humans; the Chinese thunder god, Lei Gong, portrayed as a bird man; and the Sirens of Greek mythology, who actually started out as women-bird hybrids before morphing into more familiar mermaid imagery. There are myriad other avian-human historical examples, thus underscoring the ubiquity of this imagery throughout antiquity.

Others are portrayed as possessing specific avian elements representing both species. For example, the gods Horus and Thoth from ancient Egyptian mythology were often depicted as humans with the heads of a falcon and an ibis respectively.

The bird man identified here claims he has existed since the first century. He has many secrets to reveal. "There are many on Earth who are birdlike. They possess the DNA, mindset, and thinking that of like birds. They are not able to fly nor communicate with us. Mental health facilities hold some of these strange minds. I know because I was one of them. We eat with the brain, albeit seldom and very little, and we drink water that flows from the mountains."

An additional voice surfaces, identifying itself also as bird man. "I have been chosen to tell my story, as absurd as it might seem. I was created first by Mother Nature to help populate Earth at its very beginning, along with various animals. Yes, I am a bird, and yet I am different because there are very few like me on Earth. There are others of my species on a planet where one of the Brothers experimented on us. I was fortunate because I was the first of my kind. There was much to see as man was evolving. I watched and listened closely.

"Part of my brain, as you might say, is now alien. I have good feelings for the human race and absolutely no hatred. I am neither male nor female. That is how I was created. One might say I am but a shell. However, as time went on, I grew to love those who were spirits, and they grew to love me. When they began to change, some tried to protect me before I was taken away by one of those you call the Brothers. They gave me a part of how humans developed in a transitional period.

"My brain began to develop when they gave me knowledge and understanding. Why? Perhaps because I was of the initial ones Mother Nature created and placed upon the Earth: one of the so-called first animals. Earth was truly a paradise of love at that time. But then we heard a sound like the opening of the clouds, and other spirits came forth.

"We grew to love humans, and they loved us, but Lucifer was not happy. He hated us because we were created to bring joy and love to the human race. Please bear with me, and I will try to explain in plain words what happened. They called us animals. Many hid. I was taken away by one of the Brothers and was given energy. It was not painful when it was given to me.

"I began to grow in size. Time meant nothing to me, and it meant nothing to them. Their planet is strange. I hunger for our planet. I have been given the gift of telepathic communication since you have shown me compassion and understanding. I have been saved from many tragedies. So they fear me, and do not talk about me to anyone. They are very cautious.

"All creation has been affected with a form of caring and love. All creation, even a blade of grass or single flower, has an energetic life force. It was on your planet that Mother Nature and others created us. We were to be gifts, as all of us are, to the human spirit, that which would later become male and female. We have been given a designated territory to protect. We help save people in danger of death, such as from an avalanche. They call on us because we can fly and are able to identify where people are trapped. We have saved many, but very few words are spoken about us.

"Unfortunately, Lucifer didn't give us energy to continue. When they find us now, they torture us and hide us where no one can see. They don't wish to be seen with us. People are frightened yet awed when they do see us. No sound comes from our beak, but there is a sound that penetrates their minds. If they are open to it, they will understand. Because I was the first one to be experimented on and given more pure energy, I am more attuned to what is happening. My nose, eyes, and mouth are more humanlike.

"I have come to tell you the story of our lives. We do not eat, and rarely do we rest. Divine energy keeps us alive. As I was the first, I shall also be the last when time ends for Earth. I know I shall be able to go before the Creator to explain that we do not hate, denounce, nor fear Him. We love Him."

Sasquatch/Bigfoot, Yeti, Abominable Snowman

Another subject of a Brother commenced explaining the origin of the creatures here on Earth called Sasquatch (Bigfoot) and yeti. "Let me tell you about the one you call Bigfoot." This refers directly to the various sightings of Sasquatch/Bigfoot, yeti, the Abominable Snowman, and like creatures across the globe. And it warrants further research.

"Sasquatch" has arguably become the most universally accepted name for this primate/person hybrid. The name itself is derived from the Halkomelem (i.e., the language of various First Nations peoples of the Pacific Northwest Coast) dialectal word *sésquac*, meaning "wild man." These indigenous people inhabited the Fraser Valley in the Pacific Northwest and parts of Vancouver Island, British Columbia. These two regions have yielded more recorded Sasquatch sightings than anywhere else.

The name "bigfoot," however, only dates from 1958. That was when Gerald Crew, a resident of Del Norte County, California, was pictured in the *Humboldt Times* holding the cast he made of large footprints found near his bulldozer. Fellow Bluff Creek locals began referring to the mysterious maker of the tracks as "bigfoot," which *Humboldt Times* editor, Andrew Genzoli, decided to stylize as "bigfoot."

Crossing the globe, we encounter a similar creature known as yeti, often conflated as the Abominable Snowman. The yeti is believed to be an entirely different entity from Sasquatch. Its origin can be traced back to pre-Buddhist Eastern civilizations, primarily in the Himalayan Mountain region. Unlike Sasquatch, who is most frequently spotted in warm or mild climates, the yeti is believed to be an Arctic creature usually described as resembling a bear more than an ape. The yeti was also called the "Glacier Being" by early Himalayan cultures and was worshipped as a supernatural entity. The important aspect here is that these are different creatures, underscoring their origination as alien experiments carried out by followers of the Brothers.

The channeled entity explains, "He [Sasquatch and/or yeti] is beginning to change. Some are very loving. Others are true warriors. They can smell a human being from a mile away. They are angry at the Brothers for experimenting on them. He has appeared with other older and younger beings who have not changed since the Brothers placed them on the top of a high mountain with snow on it. They live in a state of limbo. His golden chest is covered with fur. There are many like them all over creation."

The origins of these exceptional entities are explained as follows: "We are not totally human nor totally someone's creation. We exist because the Brothers gave us energy and placed us here on Earth, where we will be found at the prescribed time. We will be awakened and know it is time to stop hiding. They took humans and tried to reproduce them but could not do what was required."

Another member of this group holds a golden book titled *The Book of Life* (also known as the Akashic records). He explains some of this information is contained in this book, "It holds knowledge of how we were created, endowed with part of the human race, but never to return to Earth in such form. We do not eat flesh, nor do we drink blood as others do. We hide our secrets within our fur. Many mysteries will be revealed slowly about layers within the Earth, soon to be discovered."

These beings were created with energy taken from human beings who had been sent to another planet. Their general physical form has not changed, but what was taken from their minds cannot be replaced. They can transform between physical or spiritual instantiation. This being has something like a heart with a beautiful red glow, but with spikes all over it. It pulsates and gives energy to all in the lair to keep them alive. They too will be called back at the very end to be judged, but not until they have been returned to their original form.

Some are also awakening on the other planets to which they were sent and now want to return to Earth. They have scrambled recollections because they were implanted with different memories and feelings from different parts of an animal's brain. Fortunately, it was done without any bleeding. It was also done in the opposite direction, transforming from a human's brain into an animal. They cannot speak but are able to communicate telepathically. When they first came to Earth, they communicated entirely through the mind.

The Little People

According to Michael Furtman in his book *Magic on the Rocks*, published by Birch Portage Press in 2000, native peoples of North America told legends of a race of "little people" who lived in the woods near sandy hills; other times near rocks located along large bodies of water, such as the great lakes. Often described as "hairy-faced dwarfs" in stories, petroglyph illustrations portray small creatures with horns on their head and traveling via canoe in small groups.

There is a millennium timeline of "little-people" reports. European cultures have been replete with "little-people" mythology, tales, and legends. Ireland boasts of leprechauns; Scotland possesses brownies; German lore speaks of dwarves and kobolds; Belarussian mythology includes Zlydzens.

The South American region stretching from northeast Argentina, northward through the whole of Paraguay, and into southern Brazil, is home to the Guarini, an indigenous people of South America. Guarini culture speaks of the Pombéro, a mythical humanoid creature of small stature. As with most cultural depictions of "little people," they are perceived as mischievous creatures.

Of great interest to this channeled revelation is the tale of Sri Lanka's Nittaewo. According to the oral traditions of the Veddha tribe of Sri Lanka, and captured and recorded by Frederick Lewis in 1914, the Nittaewo were approximately three feet (1 meter) tall. Females were shorter than males. They walked erect, had no tails, and were completely naked. Their arms were short, with talon-like nails. They lived in trees, caves, and crevices, and caught and ate small animals such as hare, squirrel, and tortoise.

They lived in groups of ten or twenty, and their speech was like the twittering of birds. They fought constantly with the Veddha.

Legend has it that when they began to take Veddha children, the Veddha trapped the Nittaewo in a cave, blocked its entrance with a wood fire, killing them all—an account recorded in 1887 by British explorer, Hugh Nevill.

This coincides with revelations that female adults of various ages have been shrunk in size. They now look like a three- or four-year-old child. They have the minds of an adult and can reason; some more so than others. All their organs have been changed in some way. They will not grow any younger or older. They do not eat or drink anything and can be found all over the world. Their actual numbers remain unknown.

One of the little people speaks, "The Brothers never thought of us, or even the Heavenly Father, as important. We are not like them. That is why they watched us from the time we were spirits until we transitioned into a physical form. Lucifer is the one who fostered this change, wanting to defy the Heavenly Father, and to show how much more powerful he was than Him. Lucifer himself had no desire to be physical other than through projecting a spiritual image to be admired. He wants to supplant the Heavenly Father and rule the universe."

They do not fully understand their situation because the emotion of sadness was removed from their brains. They simply exist, and do not remember anything from their past life. They have no feelings. Their strange-looking bodies appear to be lumpy. Except for specific identifying features, physically, they are all alike.

The essential knowledge to be gleaned from these revelations is that we, humans, are not the only sentient life on Earth. The creatures described above may hide from us, but they do walk among us. While it sounds like science fiction, it isn't.

We have reason to believe that every civilization, at some time in its history, has experimented on human beings. And that all this was inspired by Lucifer. He sought to change spiritual forms into physical beings, all for the devious purpose of controlling us. In that way, we can enact his evil deeds, fulfilling his desire to both denigrate and usurp the Heavenly Father.

On each of these exile planets, there is a "specimen" who can tell the story of those who do not eat or drink. They hide together in groups, usually in warmer climates. Their long hair covers the scars on their skulls, evidence of their having undergone experimentation. They do not speak to one another. They simply exist. They do not even think about one another. Their lot is to remain together until the final judgment.

Some are monitored by followers of the Brothers. Others remain, die there, and then come back to life. Still, others return to their home planets. Regardless, the Brothers desperately want to make sure those who underwent experimentation do not reveal what happened to them. Such secrets manifest on Earth will be discovered in the future through developing technology. We do not know when, but much will be revealed.

Valley of Death

Another man who wants to tell his story is part human, animal, and alien. He already had a brilliant mind when he was taken. He is not angry about being exiled on a planet with others like him. He takes comfort from having learned so much. He strongly disagrees with the explanation the Brothers give for what they did to him.

"I was taken by an alien on a hot summer day. It was odd, but there was no fear in me. I didn't, and couldn't, fight back. It was like I was being led by someone I didn't know, but who was kind and caring. It was quite different when I entered the place where they perform the experiments. The way they dressed was strange. I could only see their eyes and hands, which were different from mine. They began to pull me apart, but I didn't cry out because I had no pain.

"When it was over, one of them removed his mask. I think it was a male. His lips never moved, but I heard him speak telepathically. He said, 'We are an experimental group. You did not fight us because you could not, but I see that you are a very intelligent person. I have not taken from you as much as I could have. I have left a part of your memory intact.

'No one believes me, but I believe in time your people will know what we have been doing. There is an old saying among us that I believe to be true: "You have no right to take from another species."' They are clueless to what they are doing and why. It seemed like he gave me some of his energy, and I slept deeply and peacefully.

"When I awoke, I was in a different place. I could not move but could see others like me. They were neither human nor animal, perhaps somewhere in between. I saw them beginning to change and wondered if I would too. I can't even describe those who were becoming more animallike. Did they know what was happening? I don't know. They never cried out. My mind kept growing even as I knew I could not return to live on Earth.

"He was a good person, this alien. He was the first of his kind to provide his own energy to a human being taken as an adult. And he seemed to experience pleasure from this action. He saw me more than just an experiment. Consequently, he shared some of his energy with me so I would not lose all manner of understanding. Then they watched us develop. Sadly, some died after becoming stone-like. Now they seem to just exist, even as part of them continues to grow. Believe me, their assurances of no longer abducting anyone from Earth are lies.

"Even though I am locked in this body, I have the privilege of being a part of the one who saved me. What he knows, I know, and hope to be able to tell more. Evil fills the core of your planet. I will try to tell you about those who have been placed back on your planet by the Brothers.

"I am not evil. There are many more on your planet like me who are able to communicate with one another. It is the time to find them, but I am unable to leave this planet. If I had, I would have died. My mind and various organs would have dried out from the experiments. Here, at least, I am safe.

"I questioned why the Heavenly Father didn't stop this. He probably doesn't want to see how cruel human beings and aliens can be, but he saw it. I can't travel physically to Earth, but I can travel in my mind. Pray for me. I know that in some strange way, you love me."

He recounts his story verbally because, for some unknown reason, the aliens did not remove the portion of his brain that controls the voice box. He knew the man who saved him was taking a chance because he saw a brilliant light in his mind. The person on each planet who was in charge of the experiments on human beings had never touched the part of man's mind that radiated, that shone. They did not know what it was. They knew instinctively to leave it alone, believing it might be part of the Heavenly Father's love for that person. Or a reflection of the soul, maybe the source, the repository of free will.

We do know souls in the first contingent of human seeds given to Lucifer were marked with this light. They seemed to be the only group who received it or on whom it was detectable. It remains on them all their incarnations and may very well inspire them to accomplish significant good. It seems to be a sign of excellence.

He explained that he had many lives before they took him. They used his sperm to create other forms of life. He was not afraid but wanted the world to know of their existence. His superiors discovered what he had done and subsequently banished him to what is called the "Valley of Death"—the place where experimented beings are sent. He says he will try to reveal more of the truth of what was—and still is—happening.

The only hope for these malformed specimens might be to return to Earth in a spiritual form, leaving their experimented physical manifestations behind. We must first ask ourselves, "Could they live here considering our atmosphere is so different from what they now experience?" The bigger question may very well be, "Would they even want to?" This is because they are asking telepathically, "Who are you? Are you evil?" They do not know us or our intentions, despite our shared origins. They do not remember what life was like on Earth.

Whenever one of these human beings who have been abducted and undergone experimentation "dies," he or she will again return to the Heavenly Father as originally determined, to be renewed in a fully human form. That person will live out whatever was to be their last life before the final judgment.

Conclusion: Mystery and Sacredness of Human Life

There is so much mystery in life that has not yet been revealed, but in the near future, we should anticipate enlightenment. When humanity begins to travel into deep space, it may or may not find the planets inhabited by these unfortunate souls. If we did happen upon them, there is a risk that we could unintentionally kill them with the viruses we unwittingly carry. Similar to the scourge early European explorers unwittingly visited upon the native populations of America.

As it turns out, these experiments on human beings is causing great collateral pain and suffering on those planets where these experiments were performed and specimens exiled. It is the result of the virus some subjects brought back from Earth. The Brothers tried to protect themselves, but their subjects kept wanting to travel to Earth. Some wanted to return home, but others wanted to remain on the earth. Negative and destructive energies have been released into their atmospheres as well as ours. As a result, the Brothers are becoming angry and distrustful of one another.

Angels give energy to one another and are very, very important. They were never like the spirits we were. They have a different form of energy, different even from the Brothers. Some aliens are beginning to experience feelings they never had before. They know now how human beings and animals feel when hurt. Their fascination and curiosity about human life has increased. This is a significant change, because in the past, they seemed to exist and function without any emotional feelings. They wonder if these transformations are the result of a virus. And, in this preponderance, their suspicions alight rightly on Lucifer.

They recognize Earth is a far different place than any of their four planetary systems. The Brothers continue to discover how life on their planets has been corrupted by Lucifer's influence. They were surprised to discover how much their subjects appear programmed, so very unlike humanity. In response, they have looked for ways to work together against him. This is so disturbing to the Brothers that they have come together to discuss this shared concern. In doing so, they have overcome much of the misunderstanding they had about their fifth brother, our Heavenly Father.

The Brothers, for the first time, have begun to disagree with one another over the "Earth people"—as some refer to us. They believed human beings did not possess much intelligence and were of little value. The awakening experienced by the specimens is of great concern to the Brothers because they never want to admit failure as per their "Book of Rules."

They are beginning to understand that they will be held accountable for what they have done. They argue they gave greater knowledge to some of those they took—that the experiments were not simply about genetic manipulation. They wanted to learn what man would do with additional knowledge.

The four Brothers have declared together their innocence, that they should not be condemned for what they did. They truly did not believe their actions to be wrong. Their justification is that they were making life better for human beings. Yet, despite our (and celestial) protestations, they are still performing experiments on us. They invoke the same excuses justifying invasion of our brains, seeking to alter our thinking processes. On a more positive note, the Brothers have manipulated the brains of animals to increasingly become our helpers. This is in accord with the divinely inspired original intention. Like humans, however, some animals will turn against us while others will be our friends.

What Is Our Future?

We have come to believe we have been given free will to do whatever we want. Why should we experiment only on mice and rats? Unscrupulous scientists are inspired to do what they want on whoever they want, especially human beings. This has been happening for years.

Ready excuse for all these actions is that our planet—and we human beings—were never supposed to exist. That might indeed be true since our existence does not appear to have been part of the original divine plan. Fact is, without us, there may truly have been perfect peace throughout the universe, throughout all creation. Conception would have ended with the four Brothers. Maybe even before them. In some cases, the divine plan did not seem to be the last word. We do not always know why. It may be our lack of intelligence. Revelation, however, is God's way of leading us to truth.

Evil will be very strong far into the future. Good men will still try to overturn evil, but the world will continue its rapid decline. As we speak, there is a group experimenting with food modification, seeking to create drugs aimed at making humans unable to think for themselves, to appear thoughtless, languid, and irresponsible.

Man will increasingly grow food in water-storage units. After achieving a certain age, people will not be permitted to live any longer. There will be enforced euthanasia, with people being given drugs to die. People will be marked so as to identify us. Many experiments will be conducted on humans. Brains will be combined. Lucifer will be behind it all.

The blood sacrifices of the past will begin again as it was when mankind originally craved blood. Once more, women will only have children for their blood. The cells of a child will be combined with those of an animal. Lucifer is using blood to cloud man's mind.

This has already been undertaken by the Brothers who believed they were more highly developed and intelligent than humans. Human bodies and minds will once again be altered. Higher beings will be judged harshly for allowing this to happen.

One country has used a mist-like drug on its people to affect them in harmful ways. Furthermore, medical professionals throughout the world are experimenting on (and with) various parts of the human body, akin to what those on other planets have done. Some of them were still alive; others were already deceased.

These researchers are motivated by the desire to make humans stronger, while simultaneously seeking greater control over us, albeit for their own purposes. Many are inspired or driven by the false curiosity Lucifer has implanted in their brains. Ultimately, those living will suffer recompense for the sins of the many before them.

What we can glean from all these revelations is that cycles of evil perpetuate themselves throughout creation. Consequently, how would we answer questions concerning and considering our own sinfulness? What evil have we done in the name of God? We too can find or conjure answers to justify the wrongs we have committed, just as the Brothers have done.

The celestial being, Him, knows the prescribed time when human existence will end. When it will return to Him. Because of our free will, though, He allows man to propagate good and evil. Some of the Brothers know about this plan, even when it will initiate. The Brothers have intervened and manipulated the brains of animals so that they will increasingly become our helpers, in accord with the original intention.

Like humans, however, some will turn against us while others will be our friends. In a break from their prior abstinence of personal intervention, some of the Brothers will seek to help the good people on Earth. They will no longer hide but will seek to communicate directly with us. Earth will not be habitable until one of the Brothers comes and cleanses it. Then, humanity will be able to live on it once again.

There will come a time in the future when Earth's waters will overflow the existing shores. Lucifer will laugh at what has happened, even as many of his followers will drown. This great loss of life will cause him severe pain and great difficulty because he will no longer have as many people to continue his evil deeds.

The revelations revealed in *The Story of Creation*, reiterated now in this book and most likely in additional works, alert us to the prospect there may be further surprises in this ever-evolving story of salvation. It seems to be a part of the unfolding essence of Truth. We can be absolutely certain that human beings do not, at present, possess full existential knowledge of the divine plan.

Epilogue to Book 2

The revelations of Connie Ann Valenti contained first in *The Stories of Creation* and in this second book, are, for many, difficult to hear, comprehend, understand, and accept. But such has been the case with revelations throughout time. St. John's Book of Revelations remains one of the most intriguing, baffling, eloquent, yet mysterious odes ever written—one pondered over daily by religious scholars, authors, mystics, and lay people.

Such is, and will be, the case, undoubtedly, with the revelations presented by Connie Ann Valenti. Within the more mystical revelations revealed, there are myriad aspects of her revelations that align significantly with human ontology, social history, the dynamic story of humanity, perceptions of good versus evil, and the challenge of being a creature endowed with free will immersed within a divine plan.

Book 2 of Connie Ann Valenti's revelations elaborates and deepens the revelations of the initial text: *The Story of Creation*. But it also presents startling new insights into the complex cosmic relationships between the celestial progeny of The One, i.e., the Creator of All. These revelations divulge a universe existing in both material and spiritual form, not just between the seen and unseen. The extended progeny of The One exist primarily in spiritual form, while those of us inhabiting Earth are souls/spirits in physical incarnation, each for an express purpose and gifted with the potential for spiritual growth and evolution. It is a complex relationship, but one more reflective of what it means to be created in God's image than we may have ever imagined.

Most religions posit humanity as being created in the image of God, i.e., The One. For millennia, this has been reflected upon in hopes of understanding exactly what it means—usually without tangible understanding. For example, are we to presume that God possesses a body similar to ours? Our Lord, Jesus Christ, reminds us firmly that God is spirit. For all the images of a mighty deity seated on a golden throne, endowing God with a physical body seems entirely antithetical to that pronouncement. It is possible, however, to presume that the functions assigned to our bodily organs and myriad functions of our planet are tangible expressions of The One's spiritual powers: the flow of life-sustaining energy, the respiration of spiritual breath, the cleansing of impurities, the gift of procreation and regeneration, artistic creation, the ability to choose certain actions within parameters of good and evil, and more. Our greatest challenge, perhaps, is reconciling being free will-gifted spirits incarnated by our Creator for the purpose of returning to unity with this very same Creator.

This is where Connie Ann Valenti's revelations seem most understandable. These revelations are supported by events, circumstances, and ontological realities existing throughout human history. It might be best for us to reach back into the very origins of western philosophy as manifested in ancient Greek civilization. The western world has always held early Greek civilization in the highest esteem. In fact, the era referred to as the Renaissance was essentially a reintroduction of Greek and Roman classical knowledge into what had been deemed the Dark Ages. So let's review exactly what this ancient knowledge was that needed to be reborn.

Our familiarity with Greek civilization focuses very much on its mythology and how this mythology ordered society and human actions. For simplicity's sake, we can explain Greek mythology in the following manner:

The world is born out of what the Greeks called "chaos." This chaos was essentially an existential nothingness, albeit vast and, in some degree, substantive. Out of this chaos is spawned Gaia (the Earth) and a host of other primary divine beings. The key verb here is "spawned" i.e., an act of procreation. The progeny of this procreation encompasses eros (love), the abyss (Tartarus), and Erebus, a primordial deity, representing the personification of darkness.

(Hesiod's Theogony identifies him as one of the first "five" beings in existence, born of chaos.) The divine being known as Gaia gave birth to Uranus (the Sky or the Heavens) but does so without male assistance. It is essentially a virgin birth or, if we wish to be scientific, parthenogenesis.

Uranus, her offspring, in turn fertilizes Gaia. And from that first union is born a veritable litter of divine entities that come to be known as the Titans. The Titans are composed of an equal number of male and female siblings. The six brothers are Coeus, Crius, Cronus, Hyperion, Iapetus, and Oceanus; the six sisters are Mnemosyne, Phoebe, Rhea, Theia, Themis, and Tethys.

The youngest of the six brothers was Cronus. Cronus becomes arguably the most famous of the Titans as he was king and leader of his brothers, fighting against Uranus and eventually the Olympian gods. Born of Uranus and Gaia, he was the wiliest and youngest of their offspring, but also arguably the most powerful.

Although Gaia commanded no more beings be born, Uranus continued to force himself upon her and further beings were created. These included the cyclops: Brontes, Steropes and Arges; and the Hecatoncheires ("hundred-handed ones"): Cottus, Briareus, and Gyges. Fearful of the power possessed by these additional offspring, Uranus throws them into Tartarus (i.e., the abyss).

This made Gaia so furious she convinces Cronus, her youngest son, to castrate his father, Uranus. He does so and becomes ruler of the Titans, and makes his sister, Rhea, his consort. His siblings comprise a supernatural royal court.

From here, Greek mythology becomes ever more severe and, we could even say, demented. The guilt of betraying his father and fear of such acts being visited upon him, causes Cronus to devour each of the children he procreates with his sister, Rhea. This continues until Rhea, disgusted by this continual infanticide, hides their child, Zeus, offering Cronus instead a blanket containing a stone in place of the child. Almost a precursor to the story of Moses, Zeus is spared and raised in a far-off land, supposedly the island of Crete.

Although devoured, these offspring were not destroyed. Rather, they remained captive within Cronus. When Zeus was full grown, and in accord with the wishes of his mother, Rhea, he fed Cronus an emetic (i.e., a medicine or substance which causes vomiting). This caused Cronus to expel forth Rhea's other children, i.e., Zeus' siblings: Poseidon, Hades, Hestia, Demeter, and Hera, as well as the stone which had been sitting in Cronus' spiritual stomach all this time.

In a vast war called the Titanomachy, Zeus and his older siblings (with the help of the Hecatoncheires and Cyclops) overthrew Cronus and the other Titans. The victorious Zeus then cuts up and casts Cronus and the Titans down to imprisonment in Tartarus (the abyss).

If there is one overriding theme to be gleaned from this panoply of Greek mythology is that of conflict. While originally father-son conflict, it devolves into all manner of incest, sibling rivalry, betrayal, fratricide, infanticide, usurpation, and more. Zeus, in fact, would replicate his own father's infanticidal delusions. After a prophecy that the offspring of his first wife, Metis, would give birth to a god "greater than he," Zeus promptly swallowed her. She was, however, already pregnant with Athena, who subsequently bursts forth from Zeus' head—fully-grown and dressed for war. And thus begins an entirely new era of familial conflict.

If we de-anthropomorphize these celestial entities and glance instead at the material universe, we find a similar degree of volatility, elemental conflict, constructs and deconstruction, and all manner of radical change and evolution. The composition of the Milky Way galaxy alone, of which we are discovering amazing new scientific understanding daily, is comparable to the cast of any Shakespearean tragedy. For example, let us examine the recent discovery that super-massive black holes can form very quickly over very short periods beyond those black holes emerging from the center of a massive star collapsing in upon itself. This is destruction and rebirth on a universal scale.

We can extend this inquiry to the fecund theory postulated by physicist, Lee Smolin, published in 1992 and summarized in his book, *The Life of the Cosmos*. Put succinctly, the fecund theory postulates that black holes cause the emergence of a new universe on the "other side." These new universes replicate fundamental constant parameters (i.e., masses of elementary particles, Planck constant, elementary charge, and so forth), differing in some ways from the universe where the black hole collapsed. By this reasoning, each universe gives birth to as many new universes as it has black holes. This is reincarnation on a universal scale.

Whereas Smolin does not definitively exclude or reject religion or mysticism, he believes science should only deal with that of which is observable. Connie Ann Valenti's revelations, however, indicate active supernatural involvement, investment, manipulation, and, at times, infestation of our spiritual and physical universe. It all becomes a question of causality: Is there a "what" causing it, a "who" causing it, or perhaps both?

We credit the ancient Greeks with incredible insight into their physical world. They acquired knowledge about myriad subjects—much of it prescient, much of it ultimately revised throughout time. Rome considered Greece so advanced it adopted and absorbed many of its customs and gods. For too long, the attempt by the ancient Greeks to understand the origins of the world, time, and the ontological dynamics of human interaction have been dismissed as pure fantasy, consigned to a pagan past. But suppose the Greeks and other ancient civilizations had more than an inkling that the supernatural realm was indeed governed and created by different supernatural entities and that these entities exhibit many—if not all—of the behaviors attributed to humanity, then let us suppose the Greeks believed these entities continued to impact and influence human behavior.

What might we glean from this genealogy of divine spiritual conflict? How might we relate all this to the revelations provided to Connie Anne Valenti, made known via these written works?

First, these revelations reinforce the notion of a supernatural hierarchy. In fact, these revelations infer an imperial hierarchy of celestial beings, reflecting the imperial history of much human civilization. An imperial hierarchy implies the existence of an emperor, namely a sovereign ruler of great power and rank, one ruling an empire. What then is an empire? The territorial domain and population of an empire is a sovereign state functioning as an aggregate of nations or people, commonly of greater extent than that of kingdoms. It is consequently ruled over by an emperor or another form of imperial monarch. Our spiritual empire is ruled by a truly omniscient, omnipotent, divine being called The One.

Within human history there have been myriad empires. Interestingly enough, only one remains today: Japan. Perhaps our world's familiarity with emperors owes more to *Star Wars* than history books. In that fictional galaxy of Star Wars, Emperor Palpatine (a.k.a. Darth Sidious) possesses supernatural powers, albeit for the "Dark Side"—a personification of evil incarnate. Emperor Palpatine is the diametrical opposite of everything we know about The One, who, if we take our cue from popular culture, is the embodiment of the Light Side of the Force. Ironically, this is a most appropriate title since a given attribute of The One and his creations is that they exist as and in uncreated light.

What history reveals about imperial hierarchies is that individual realms exist within them. Kaiser Wilhelm was emperor of a united Germany, consisting of multiple kingdoms and principalities. As emperor though, he was the true head of state with the power to overrule the lesser monarchs. These kingdoms grew out of and coalesced around specific familial groupings. Even today, monarchs are often denoted by their national origins. For example, Philippe is King of the Belgians; Elizabeth II is Queen of the United Kingdom of Great Britain, Northern Ireland, and her other realms and territories. Sovereignty and geography go together. This idea becomes of paramount importance as we contemplate the vastness of the universe—a universe of which we are but one infinitesimal part.

So we have within human history and societal organization myriad examples of imperial structure. If this societal structure existed on Earth and throughout human history, who is to say the original blueprint wasn't celestial and spiritual?

As Americans, there is an intrinsic repulsion to monarchy, seeing that our country was birthed by rebellion against an absolute monarch, namely George III. As Christians though, we are implicit monarchists, viewing our Father as divine royalty. We also recognize our Father as being served by a hierarchy of angels. It has been postulated that our Father is served by three distinct spheres of angels. The first sphere is comprised of seraphim, cherubim, and thrones. The second sphere is comprised of dominions, virtues, and powers; while the third sphere is comprised of principalities, archangels, and angels. They are essentially a royal court.

Five thousand years ago, according to the Jewish calendar, clarification was provided regarding the celestial and spiritual oversight of Earth, when God—who we would soon call our Heavenly Father by decree of his incarnate son, Jesus Christ—appeared to patriarch Abraham and announced himself as "I Am Who I Am." Part of his intent was to remove the confusion manifested in human minds by the awareness of—but false understanding of—the true role of this spiritual hierarchy in the affairs of humankind and this planet.

How pervasive was this event? It confirmed our Earth as the domain of a single entity within the spiritual hierarchy, thus making us monotheistic. It is important to note that Abraham is described both in the Tanakh and the Quran, and is recognized by Jews, Christians, Muslims, and others. This was the beginning of true revelation about our place in the divine schema and established our reliance on the spiritual entity serving as our God.

Through Connie Ann Valenti's revelations, we learn of the origins of our Father; the creation of the Archangel Lucifer; his fall from grace, resulting from many of the seven deadly sins; the offering of the Archangel Jesus/Mary; the salvation of humanity; and the ongoing challenges of being spiritual beings capable of multiple temporal existences for the express purpose of learning great, essential truths.

Additionally, we hail Jesus Christ as our spiritual king, commanding legions of angels, saintly souls, and devout, devoted incarnate humans. If Jesus is our king, replacing the soiled Lucifer for whom Earth was created, might our Father be emperor of his designated spiritual/incarnate domain?

The demise of earthly empires leads one to contemplate the rise of democracy. Democracy means basically rule by the people. It is the supplanting of divine right by individual choice. Choice leads to the power of individuals to choose freely. It implies a specifically granted or guaranteed power to choose a desired option, alternative, preference, selection, moral imperative, as well as the desire, actions, and opportunity to dehumanize, demonize, and choose overall negation. The revelations of Connie Ann Valenti underscore free will as the greatest attribute given to humanity; that our endowment with free will has inadvertently initiated an entire reordering of both the universe and its spiritual realms.

It makes sense to revisit the classic Baltimore Catechism of the Roman Catholic Church to understand the challenges posed to free will. In that regard, we need to examine what has been referred to, historically, as the seven deadly sins. The revelations of Connie Ann Valenti may be giving us tremendous insight into the origin of those vices that have come to make human existence so challenging. The seven deadly sins are gluttony, greed, sloth, wrath, envy, lust, and pride. Were they solely designed attributes of humanity or might they actually constitute part of our divine DNA, hard as that might be for some to imagine or believe?

Even our planet exudes chemical and elemental conflict. Tectonic plates generating the friction-seeding volcanoes, earthquakes, tsunamis, thermal vents, and more. Perhaps all this was and is part of both celestial and human DNA. These revelations indicate many of these "sins" as a genuine reflection of divine relationships and interaction. What does become certain is that there is a genuine desirable ultimate goal to human existence, and it involves a power beyond human comprehension, namely love. Love is as profound on a spiritual level as the effect of gravity in the material world.

Connie Ann Valenti's revelations also inadvertently confirm one of the most recent and radical theories in physics, namely string theory. I say "inadvertently" because Connie Ann Valenti has no knowledge whatsoever of string theory. String theory suggests that the fundamental constituents of the universe are one-dimensional "strings" rather than point-like particles. It posits that all fundamental particles are actually one-dimensional, string-like entities whose vibrations determine the particles' properties, such as their mass and charge. String theory also requires six or seven extra dimensions of space and contains ways of relating large extra dimensions to small ones.

This is groundbreaking in that it transcends our naturally perceived three dimensions of space—length, width, and depth—and the one dimension of time. If there are many more dimensions, and one leading physics model of the last half century proposes as many as ten dimensions, then suddenly everything from sci-fi warp drive, to the ability to travel throughout the universe via consciousness, to interdimensional communication (including with those who have departed the Earthly plane) becomes more than just conceivable. Furthermore, the emphasis string theory puts on vibration as the determining factor for an entities' qualities and attributes resonates with many spiritually channeled texts of recent times, especially the spiritual guides (who identify themselves with Melchizedek) of Paul Selig's oeuvre.

Lastly, these revelations also explain the perplexing and confounding interactions that have occurred between humanity and alien entities. Connie Ann Valenti's revelations confirm the existence of other sentient forms in the universe; forms that are and can be both spiritual and material. She traces these alien encounters back to the spiritual progeny of the great imperial court that created our universe and potentially other universes. In doing so, she reveals sibling rivalries as profound as any found in ancient Greek mythology.

For centuries, there have been historical recordings of alien encounters as well as abductions. One consistent theme among the vast majority of these alien encounters is basic curiosity and intrigue regarding human beings as a distinct species of sentient existence.

Connie Ann Valenti's revelations explain the relationship between aliens and humans in a number of illuminate ways. First, she reveals we are all related by virtue of being progeny of a band of related supernatural siblings of which our Heavenly Father is the youngest. Bluntly speaking, these "aliens" are actually our cousins. This might explain why descriptions of them very much resemble human physiognomy.

Connie Ann Valenti's revelations ground this curiosity in the fact that humanity has been endowed with the unique gifts of free will (unlike our alien cousins) and the ability to volitionally propagate (which alien races are unable to do). Consider it curiosity born out of jealousy.

We now understand that alien experimentation has been, at times, haphazard attempts at discerning and discovering the keys to these human attributes in hopes of imbuing them into their own cultures. We learn that our alien cousins, while technologically advanced, are not immune from serious motivational weaknesses. As a result, there have occurred salacious alien experimentation akin to the worst human experimental atrocities occurring at Nazi concentration camps during World War II. The reasoning behind these alien perversions can only find consistency within the warped reasoning of Lucifer, a nefarious viral motivation we learn is now extending well beyond Earth.

It is for you to decide whether this is all just coincidence or revelation as answer, confirmation, and proof the Greeks and many other "primitive" civilizations were in fact not so primitive but actually on to something. They were just born too soon to understand and see the truths now revealed.

About the Author

Donald Marinelli has been an educator for over forty years. He has taught previously at Carnegie Mellon, Arizona State University, Columbia University, and other colleges and universities. He is cofounder and past executive director of the Carnegie Mellon University Entertainment Technology Center, one of the first true right brain-left brain initiatives in higher education.

A lifelong futurist, Dr. Marinelli believes art, science, and faith share fundamental foundations—that technology is the pinnacle of artistic creation. He is a believer in a universe more complex than human imagination has yet envisioned. Dr. Marinelli has known Connie Ann Valenti for decades, has observed and witnessed the insight and impact of her revelations, such that he believes there is great value in considering what is revealed in *The Story of Creation* and these later revelations.

He is the author of the book, *The Comet and the Tornado*—his recounting of his years working with the late Dr. Randy Pausch of "The Last Lecture" fame.